A New Way of Thinking about Yourself

When I was twenty-seven, I came to a crisis in my life. I had everything I thought I wanted—a wife, a job teaching drama at a prestigious university. Yet I found myself going through periods of deep depression, periods when nothing I was doing seemed to give me any pleasure or even make any sense.

The problem was that I was *acting* my life, not living it. Nothing seemed real to me. I was so worried about being a good teacher and a good husband that I completely lost sight of who I was and what really made me happy.

The process of getting myself unstuck took several years, but looking back on it, I can see that it was really very simple: I stopped holding myself back. I stopped trying so hard. I learned to let go and enjoy myself, to surrender to the act of living, rather than worry so much about results and what other people thought.

Through the techniques I will be describing, I learned to give up the need to "perform," and ironically my performance in every area of my life improved a thousand-fold. You too can gain access to inner resources that will free you from self-imposed restraints and from dependence on other people for approval.

I have written this book around the actual stories of six of my students who have found in my workshop the keys to joyful self-acceptance and full personal expression.

Join them now on this liberating journey.

—*Bret Lyon*

THE BRET LYON PERSONAL POWER PROGRAM

by Bret Lyon, Ph.D.

MEDALLION BOOKS · LOS ANGELES

THE BRET LYON
PERSONAL POWER PROGRAM

Copyright © 1986 by Bret Lyon

An original Medallion Books edition, published
for the first time anywhere.

First printing, July 1986

Second printing, August 1986

ISBN: 1-55627-022-4

Cover design by Frank Mulvey

MEDALLION BOOKS, INC.
5455 Wilshire Boulevard, Suite 1700
Los Angeles, California 90036

Printed in the United States of America

To Jenny, who taught me to love again
And to the future

CONTENTS

ACKNOWLEDGMENTS

I want to thank the many students whose trust in me and willingness to risk made this book possible, especially those who recognize pieces of themselves in the following pages. Special thanks to Roberta and Michael Rey for their powerful, unfailing support; Al Bauman and Mark Waldman for all they taught me; Mary Beth Crain, who was instrumental in helping my work reach a larger audience; Nancy Schandera, who introduced me to the Science of Mind community; Lynn Walford, who suggested the format for this book; Lennie Felder, who helped so much with the manuscript; and Myra Glazer and Sierra University for helping me bring it to fruition. And to Jenny, who helped me far more than I realized—in her own quiet way. Also, to Austin Anton, Pauline Sugine, Carole Frueh, Peggy King, Joel Dweck, and Anne Ruderman for all their friendship and support.

I would like to thank my mother, Lucy, for her continued support, her willingness to accept me through my changes, and for instilling in me the belief that I could do anything I set my mind to; also my aunt, Daisy, for all that she has done for me. And I send love and best wishes to my father and sister, who have passed on—if only I could share with you all that I know now.

THE BRET LYON PERSONAL POWER PROGRAM

1

SUCCESS STORIES

When I was 27 years old, I came to a crisis in my life. I had everything that I thought I wanted: a wife, a house, a job teaching drama at a prestigious university. Yet I found myself going through periods of deep depression, when nothing I was doing seemed to give me any pleasure or even make any sense.

The problem was, as I realized several years later, that I was acting. Nothing in my life seemed real to me. I was so worried about being a good teacher and being a good husband that I had completely lost sight of what I wanted—of what made me happy.

Even though I was highly successful in my career, it all seemed a performance. Or even worse, a dress rehearsal. I couldn't commit myself fully to my teaching because I had always felt I was meant for "something better." My students all liked me, but they never got to know me. I was afraid that if I set strict standards, or if I let them know when I was angry or disappointed, they wouldn't like me anymore. And I felt that I couldn't talk to anyone else on the faculty because "they wouldn't understand."

My marriage had already collapsed under the weight of all the unexpressed resentments and the striving to live up to impossible ideals. I was afraid that if I told my wife what I really thought and felt, she wouldn't respect me anymore. Ironically, I was a drama teacher who was playing a role in everyone else's script. And I couldn't do a very good job because I kept worrying about the reviews.

Rather than being myself, I kept trying to perform in the way I thought I was supposed to. I was suffering from a case of terminal stagefright.

How did I get so stuck? My crisis at twenty-seven was the culmination of years of increasing physical and emotional tension, which prevented me from feeling my impulses and desires. As I grew more and more detached from my body and my emotions, I became more and more dependent on other people's feelings and opinions.

I have since learned that the more sure of yourself you are, the more you are your own person, the more people like and respect you. Unfortunately, back then I didn't know how to be my own person. Much as I would have liked to stop performing and start expressing myself, my own body got in the way.

I was always more comfortable with my

mind than my body. Even as a child, my body never seemed to do what I wanted it to. I was chosen last for team sports. Though I loved to sing, I couldn't carry a tune. I was politely told to mouth the words at school musicals. As bad as things had been, at puberty they became even worse. I was tormented by sensations I knew it was wrong to even *have*, let alone act out.

As I matured and shed my baby fat, I developed an athletic look that was always belied by my actual performance. At Amherst College I was the worst swimmer on the worst swimming team in college history. When the swimming coach happened to meet my mother at graduation, all he could muster up in the way of praise was, "He sure tried hard." He was right. I tried too hard. I wanted so badly to perform well that I kept tensing all my muscles and getting in my own way.

I majored in philosophy in college, still trying to achieve happiness through my mind. I received a doctorate from the Yale School of Drama and went on to a successful career in college teaching, but ten years of desperate attempts to force myself to write creatively left me with little to show but a paralyzing case of writer's block.

As my body filled with tension, my posture and movement became more and more distorted. I found this out one day when I was coming out of the Tufts University Library and

I spied one of my students coming up the path toward me. As soon as he saw me, he leaned his upper body forward, stuck his head out, hunkered down and began rolling his body from side to side. "What are you doing?" I asked. "Imitating you," he replied.

Somewhat upset, I went home and stood against the wall. My buttocks and shoulders touched, but almost nothing else did. And try as I might, I couldn't fix it. Neither my head nor the middle of my back would come anywhere near the wall. I had to accept the truth. I did stand and walk like a gorilla. And I thought there wasn't anything I could do about it.

Today, I stand straight and tall. I am often complimented on my speaking and singing voice and occasionally applauded when I dance socially. I teach now because I have come to realize how much I love to teach. Rather than working in a college, I now teach and coach privately—and my reputation, class size and income have increased beyond my wildest dreams. My students are actors and nonactors who want to learn the secrets of full self-expression. You have seen some of my acting students on TV and in films.

I am in an exciting, honest relationship which, after six years, keeps getting better and better. After years of writer's block, I now write and perform my own songs. And I have been able to write this book—and thoroughly enjoy the process.

It has been a real shock to realize, as I did recently, that I'm not scared anymore. I wake up each morning looking forward to each day with joy and excitement, waiting to see what it has to offer. Sometimes there are interesting activities that I have planned: My class, a talk show interview, a meeting about the book, lunch with a student or colleague, a trip to the mountains. Sometimes it's just the sun.

And magically, Jenny is always there, waking up beside me.

Through high school, college and my career, I never had more than one or two friends at a time. Now it seems that there are dozens, hundreds. I am collaborating with so many different people in so many different ways.

How did I change so radically? How was I able to get myself unstuck in so many areas which seemed so unchangeable? The process took me several years, but as I look back on it I can see that it was really very simple. I stopped holding myself back. I stopped trying so hard. I learned to enjoy myself and the process of living rather than worrying so much about results and what other people thought. Through the technique I will be describing in this book, I learned to live without "stagefright." Ironically, as I was able to give up the need to perform, my performance in every area of my life improved a thousandfold.

I had been teaching playwriting and dramatic criticism. As I discovered the secrets of "nonperforming," of accomplishing more by not trying, it seemed appropriate for me to begin to teach acting. I developed my theories in New York, where I built a reputation as an acting coach as well as directed over thirty plays off- and off-off-Broadway. Then I moved to Los Angeles, where my career flowered.

I was working with people who were paid—some of them extremely well paid—to be expressive. Yet these professionals had many of the same physical, vocal and emotional limitations I had observed in myself. They could become mired in the same pattern of self-doubt and trying too hard. My work proved to be extremely beneficial in helping them express their natural power and truthfulness.

One young man, whose story is told more fully further on in this book, got the lead in a feature film on his first professional audition. The director was astounded by his freedom and natural ease. Tom had been able to give up his preconceptions about "acting." He had learned to allow his impulses free rein. Through several months of studying with me, he was able to drop the "cool" act which had sustained him for nineteen years and let his emotions show. He had put time and effort into gaining the deceptive simplicity which won him the role.

Some actors could be extremely free, open and powerful onstage or in front of the camera. And yet they clammed up when they were not performing. It was as if they could only be themselves when they were acting. Many of them were only interested in my work insofar as it could help their technique. They really couldn't see their performing as a continuation of the rest of their lives. While I could respect that position, it wasn't enough for me. I felt a need to help people change as profoundly as I had changed—not only in their craft, but in their day-to-day lives.

Since my work with actors was so successful, I decided to open my classes to include everybody, nonactors as well as actors—anyone interested in freeing themselves from self-imposed restraints. This new venture succeeded beyond my wildest expectations.

Through my work, I saw people from all walks of life free their voices, bodies and emotions, break out of career and relationship ruts, give up dependencies on food, drugs and alcohol, and move on to more fulfilling ways of living. And while the changes did take time and commitment, they happened more quickly and painlessly than I would have ever thought possible.

I will be describing some of the changes in a step-by-step process over the course of this book. Let me give you two examples:

Brian was an architect at a large firm, who kept watching younger men get promoted ahead of him. Brian planned out everything, even the simplest sentence. Several months after starting my Self-Expression Workshop, Brian announced that he had gotten a promotion.

"It was easy," he said. "I didn't even have to ask. There I was, feeling so angry and resentful, and they were only waiting for me to be ready. Opportunity's been knocking on my door all along. But I've been standing with my shoulder against the door keeping it out. All I have to do is stand back and let it in."

In another month, Brian was swaggering into class. "I got another promotion," he said. "I'm a project supervisor now. But there's something even more exciting. I've just gotten my first commission to design on my own. A film studio. In Arizona." And then the capper. Brian, who had planned every word and every movement, said, "Of course, it'll be my first project on my own. And I've never even participated in designing a film studio before. But I'll just go down there and wing it. I know I can solve any problems as they come up."

Darlene, now a very successful actress, came into my class when her career was just starting to take off. She was having terrible anxiety attacks. Once she had been rushed to the hospital, unable to breathe. When I talked to her privately, it became clear that she was afraid she would leave her husband. "I'm starting to get work," she said. "I'm starting to travel. I got married when I was very young. I love my husband, but our relationship has gotten kind of safe and boring. I'm not sure I'll survive the temptation. Time apart. All those good-looking men . . ."

I shared with Darlene a statement by the psychologist Fritz Perls which had had a deep effect on me:

"Anxiety plus Oxygen equals Excitement." "Your anxiety," I explained, "is really excitement without enough oxygen to support it. You are really excited about your new situation and all the opportunities it offers. You can't accept all the excitement, so you become paralyzed with fear."

"Are you saying my fear isn't real?" Darlene asked.

"Oh, it's real enough. Fear usually comes to rest on an issue that could be a real problem, like your marriage ending. But the fear is coming up because your body can't handle the excitement. I understand your problem because I've been in the same place myself. I felt I was ready to be successful, but somehow I kept getting in my own way. Finally, I realized that my body just couldn't handle the pleasurable sensations that would come with success. It would just be too exciting."

"What did you do?" she asked.

"The same thing I'm going to teach you to do. I learned to loosen my body, breathe better, and get more oxygen."

Two months later, Darlene was radiant. She was going out of town on a film and she was tremendously excited.

"What about your marriage?" I asked her.

"Oh, there's no problem," she responded. "We've been getting along better than we ever have." Then, even though we were talking privately, she dropped her voice and leaned toward me. "Our sex life has been fantastic. Unbelievable. Better than our honeymoon. . . . I think it's all that oxygen."

What I learned and what I have been teaching for ten years now is the heart and soul of performance. Acting, singing, speaking to groups, playing sports, writing—you can only rise to excellence when you stop worrying and start enjoying the process. And enjoyment is physical as well as psychological. You have to change your body as well as your mind. The same holds true for all those areas in life in which you feel you have to perform. Where in your life do you have stagefright? Where do you feel that being yourself isn't good enough?

On the job?

In your marriage?

In bed?

With your lover?

With your boss?

With your colleagues?

With your friends?

With strangers?

In front of large groups?

In front of more than one person?

With your parents?
With your children?
With your students?

Like my classes, this book is designed to help you discover that you don't have to be "on" and performing all the time. It will show you how to gain access to your inner resources so you won't be so dependent on other people. Even in genuine performance situations, you will learn how to feel pleasure and excitement rather than anxiety.

You will gain tools for changing the situation around you. Many times, however, as I found with my career and Darlene found with her husband, it's not the outward circumstances, but your attitude toward them which will change. You may be totally fed up with your job or your relationship only to find that paradise was right under your nose.

In acting and in life, your performance is far more than the words you use. The truth is conveyed in your body, your emotions, the relaxation and certainty with which you express yourself. Similarly, learning to worry less and enjoy more involves not just your rational mind, but your total being. To repeat myself, to change your mind is not enough; you have to change your body also.

At the most basic level, I hope that my Personal Power Program will radically change your way of thinking about yourself and what it means to "perform." To achieve this, I have used the actual stories of six students who are each carefully disguised composites. While some of the circumstances have been changed, all of the incidents are real. Some of the students are actors whom you may have seen on TV or in films. Others are "ordinary people." You can follow their journey to greater self-acceptance, increased pleasure, and full self-expression.

I have also provided a series of simple exercises which emphasize a new way of doing things. Rather than planning what you want to do, then trying to do it, I would like you to allow something to happen and then discover what it is. Rather than trying to control or fix anything, your conscious mind will merely observe.

The Self-Expression Workshop provides a safe, liberating environment where my students and I can try out a wide range of body and breathing patterns, emotions and behavior. In order to get the maximum out of this book, you also need to create a safe place— both in the world and in your own mind. You will want to set aside special time to do the exercises in this book.

We are ready to begin our journey. Like any good playwright, let me set the scene and introduce you to your traveling companions:

The seven of us sat on cushions in my studio in Santa Monica. A cool breeze blew through the window, dispersing the heat of a summer day. As I looked around the room, I felt a surge of excitement. I had developed my techniques over many years of teaching college students and professionals to be better actors. But this was the first class open to the general public, where acting ability was not necessarily the goal. Could my work help people become more assertive and effective in their daily lives?

My students waited expectantly as I introduced myself. I asked them why they were here, what they expected to get out of the class. Tom spoke up first. He was a blond, good-looking young man of about twenty:

"My mother saw a flyer about this class. I've been thinking about trying to do some acting, but I haven't been able to get started. I had a course in high school. Now I'm in college and I can't get a part—even a small part. I get so nervous when I get up on stage. Also, I clown around a lot. Sometimes people tell me that I just can't be serious."

Bill spoke next. He was a distinguished-looking businessman in his mid-forties. "I saw your ad in the paper. I have to make presentations at work and they always terrify me. Also, people sometimes tell me I'm not sensitive enough about other people's feelings. I've had a few employees quit on me because of that. And my wife gets upset with me sometimes. It's like I'll say something without even realizing it and all of a sudden she's moping in a corner. Also, I tend to be too serious. Friends are always telling me to "lighten up."

"I'm not sure exactly why I'm here," said Storm, a buxom woman in her mid-thirties. Her forceful demeanor was contradicted by her little girl voice. "I guess it's my voice. It doesn't really fit me. Also, I always seem to be having trouble with men. I'm real suspicious and distrustful, and I tend to keep things to myself. I'd like to communicate better with them."

"I tend to be very timid," said June, a mousey-looking woman in her late forties. "I need to speak up. I was going to take an assertiveness training course, but I was too scared. Then I read about this class in the *L.A. Times*. I used to be an actress, believe it or not. But that was a long time ago. I was a lot more outgoing then. Sometimes I feel that I'd like to go back to acting, but I guess that's impossible. I mean, look at me now. It's funny how we change." Her face took on a sad look and her voice faded out as she finished.

June had stated a very common problem. Almost everyone can remember a time when they were more outgoing, when they expressed more of themselves. We all seem to tighten up as we get older. I hoped that I could help her reverse the process.

Duke spoke up next. He was in his early thirties, with almost matinee-idol good looks. Yet he dressed and groomed himself to make sure no one would know the truth about his appearance. Duke's face was striking, both sensitive and tough-looking, and the two qualities seemed to be at war. When he spoke, his voice was so breathy that it was hard to make out what he was saying—a sharp contrast with his imposing appearance.

"I've been interested in getting to know my body better. I've studied yoga and other Eastern disciplines. Right now, I guess I'm in a lot of confusion about making a living. I'm a writer, but I can't seem to write anything. I'm working as a carpenter, but I don't really like it and I can't really relate to the other guys. I'm in a relationship and that's giving me a lot of trouble. I guess I'm confused."

Duke's final statement produced some laughter. I could see a clear connection between that breathy, almost inaudible voice and his lack of direction.

Lisa was the last student. There was a silence as we waited for her to speak.

"I really don't want to say anything," she said. ". . . Okay, I guess I'm here because it's so hard for me to say things, and I tend to hold everything inside. I'm used to being by myself and that's much easier for me. How I got myself here I really can't imagine." She stopped as suddenly as she had begun.

However she had managed to arrive, I was glad to see her. I sensed tremendous potential under all that fear. In fact, I was pleased with all my students.

"I have a feeling we're going to have a very exciting time together," I responded. "It seems like all of you want to loosen up, to let go of anxiety and tension, and to be more spontaneous. You all have trouble getting what you want. You would like to reestablish contact with parts of yourself that you feel you've lost touch with. Tom, you want to be more serious. Bill, you want to lighten up. Storm, you want to relate better to the opposite sex. Can anyone identify with that problem?"

Everyone, including myself, raised his hand.

"I guess there's unanimity on that one. June and Lisa both want to speak up more, and Bill wants to speak up a little less. Good, we have plenty to accomplish."

"Do you really think we'll be able to make all these changes?" Storm asked.

"Absolutely," I responded. "I work by helping you become more aware of your body and your breathing in order to free them from tension. As your body and breathing begin to change, your emotional life and your behavior will change also."

"Can you really change how uptight I am just by changing my body and my breathing?" asked June.

"We'll find out," I replied.

2

FEARLESS BREATHING

Most of us spend a good deal of our time holding our breath or keeping our breathing shallow. If you don't breathe, you restrict your energy and cut yourself off from your feelings. You lose your natural rhythm of action and begin to try too hard.

Breathing is your most essential activity. As simple and basic as it is, breathing fully and freely is the first step to personal power. By helping you breathe more, I will help you reconnect with your power source. You will regain access to your feelings and impulses. How you breathe—or don't breathe—is reflected in every aspect of your life.

It is fear that keeps your breathing short and shallow: fear of feeling bad, fear of doing or saying something that will get you into trouble. As you begin to breathe more fully, you will find that the fear transforms into excitement.

The mechanics of breathing are very different from what you think they are. A full breath involves almost every muscle in the body. Breathing happens automatically. You don't have to think about it. Your body knows how to breathe. There is a special place in your brain whose only job is to regulate your breathing. You need to learn to stop controlling and thereby inhibiting your breathing; to let your breathing do what it wants to do.

Breathe Easy, Try Easy

As I began to talk to the class, I felt my body stiffen and my breathing stop.

I looked around the room and saw June looking at me, an expression of intense concentration on her face. She was obviously trying to absorb all that I was saying. Every muscle in her body was tensed with the effort of concentration. She wasn't breathing at all.

"Breathe," I told her.

Everyone took it as a command and the room suddenly felt lighter and more relaxed. With the straining of concentration, everyone had inhibited his breathing.

"How did you know I wasn't breathing?" asked June.

"Because when I looked at you, I stopped breathing," I replied. "Breathing and holding your breath are both contagious. We unconsciously pick up the breathing patterns of the people around us."

"I do notice that I hold my breath a lot," said June. "And I also tense up a lot. From what you said, I can see that the two are closely related."

"They're more than related. Tensing your muscles and holding your breath are part of the same thing—a general holding pattern which comes from trying too hard."

"What do you mean?" asked Bill.

"I'll give you an example. Pick up that pillow."

"Why?" Bill asked.

"Humor me. Pick up the pillow."

Bill picked up the pillow effortlessly and sat there holding it, looking confused.

"Good. Now put it down again and, this time, *try* to pick up."

Bill got even more puzzled. "I can't try to pick it up. I either pick it up or I don't."

"Exactly. Now imagine that the pillow is made of lead and is extremely heavy. Tom, you want to try to pick it up?"

Tom walked over to the pillow, tensed his arms and legs, took in a breath and held it and bent down. With exaggerated grunts and groans, he lifted the pillow.

"Good," I responded to his performance. "The pillow was heavy, it required effort, so you could *try* to pick it up. What did the trying involve?"

"I noticed that I tensed up. I tried to prepare my muscles," responded Tom.

"You also did something else. You sucked in your breath and held it until you started lifting. Then you started to grunt and groan, letting the breath out. Some people might actually hold their breath the entire time they were lifting."

"That's what I do," said Storm with the excitement of revelation. "I hold my breath whenever I lift anything heavy."

"There is no better way to strain your back. We are designed to keep breathing at all times. For some reason, many people hold their breath whenever they begin to try hard. You saw how naturally Bill picked up the pillow. There was no effort involved. As soon as there is difficulty, however, we change our whole pattern of breathing. In fact, we often hold our breath doing easy things, as if we want to make them difficult."

"It seems too hard to do two things at the same time," said June. "If I'm trying to concentrate on doing something difficult, I can't also pay attention to my breathing."

"But you don't have to pay attention to your breathing. It takes care of itself. That's the amazing thing. We artificially stop our breathing. *Our concept of trying hard involves tensing our muscles and holding our breath. And both actions are self-defeating.* This happens not only with physical tasks but with mental tasks—any activity which we regard as difficult."

"And by not breathing," put in June, "we make the activity even more difficult. It's a vicious cycle."

June had hit the nail exactly on the head. I have experienced the vicious cycle in my own life and have seen it many times with my students. I have also seen and experienced many instances when the cycle has been broken.

As an example, one of my friends had to take a typing test at work to get an increase in salary. Even though she could type quickly enough in a nontest situation, she kept failing the exam. By the end of the exam, she would feel so lightheaded that she was almost passing out. After the third time this happened, she told me about it. I speculated that she had probably stopped breathing. While breathing is designed to be automatic, it wasn't for her. I suggested that the next time she consciously remind herself to breathe. The next time she took the exam, she passed with ease.

I told this story to my students, closing with my rule of life: "Never try hard and always keep breathing."

"Wait a minute," said Bill. "You've got to try hard. Otherwise you'd never accomplish anything. We'd all just be sitting around loafing."

"When I was a kid playing baseball," I responded, "I used to run to first base, tensing up every muscle in my body with the effort. Of course, I was always out, but I figured I'd be thrown out anyway, and at least people could see how hard I was trying. What I've finally learned how to do, and what I will try to help you learn, is how to *keep breathing and try easy.*"

"What do you mean, 'try easy'?" asked June.

"Well, I would like to say, 'don't try at all,' but that isn't really accurate. There is a sense of purpose that we need in order to accomplish anything. What I want to avoid is the effort or strain that we usually get into—trying because we are afraid we are going to fail rather than trying because we plan to succeed. *'Trying hard' implies effort and a great deal of seriousness. 'Trying easy' implies ease and enjoyment*—and not taking the task too seriously, no matter how serious it is."

"And the key to trying easy is breathing easy," put in Tom.

"Exactly," I replied.

If You Don't Breathe, You Don't Feel

There is another important reason why many of us have developed the habit of holding our breath or keeping our breathing shallow: the less we breathe, the less we feel. The connection between breathing and the emotions is one of the great discoveries of Wilhelm Reich. Many of the explanations and exercises in my class and in this book are derived from his theories.

Reich was a disciple of Freud. In standard psychoanalysis, the patient lay on a couch and free-associated, saying whatever came into his mind. Sometimes, however, the patient would just lie there—at fifty dollars an hour—and not say anything. No thoughts would come. Freud gave Reich the task of finding some way to speed up the analysis. What Reich found was that if the patient wasn't free-associating, he also wasn't breathing—or breathing just enough to sustain life. Reich found that if he increased his breathing, the patient would start free-associating.

Reich finally broke with psychoanalysis because he was dissatisfied with the slowness of results. A person could talk for years, understand everything about his past, and still not change. In classical psychoanalysis the big thing was the primal scene, when you saw or heard your parents making love. But Reich found he could get patients to the scene and the patient would say, So? *There was no emotion attached.* If the emotions weren't affected, Reich theorized, there would be no change. So he searched for a way to affect the emotions. And he found that by increasing the breathing, he increased the emotional charge, or intensity.

As Reich continued to work, he did less verbal analysis and more work directly on the body to release muscles and free breathing.

How We Breathe

As adults, we have to relearn what we once

knew as children. We have to learn to get out
of our own way so that breathing can be full
and free. We have not only learned to restrict
our breathing, we have also learned many rules
about breathing, all of which are wrong.

The general confusion became very obvious
when I asked my students how we breathe.

"It has something to do with the diaphragm," Lisa said.

"Your lungs expand," June suggested.

"Air comes in through your nose and expands your lungs," said Duke.

"The diaphragm moves up and down."

"The chest moves."

"Doesn't something happen with the ribs?"

"Okay, let's take one thing at a time," I suggested. "The diaphragm does move. But how?"

"What is the diaphragm?" asked Bill.

"It's a muscle, isn't it?" Duke responded
tentatively.

As we didn't seem to be getting anywhere,
I decided to try our first exercise. I told my
students to take a deep breath.

Bill and Storm expanded their chests, Bill
noisily sucking in air through his mouth. Duke
and Lisa, who had both studied Yoga, expanded
their stomachs. I could hear Duke pulling in
air through his nose.

"What happens?" I asked.

"Aren't you supposed to pull in air through
your nose?" Duke asked.

"I thought you were supposed to breathe

in through your mouth and out through your nose," said Bill.

"The idea as I see it," I replied, "is to get in all the air you can as quickly as possible. If you could breathe through your ears, I would suggest doing that also."

When we breathe consciously, we actively suck air into our lungs. As the lungs expand, they can cause the diaphragm to lower. When we breathe automatically, however, the process is exactly reversed: the diaphragm lowers, providing room for the lungs to expand, creating a partial vacuum. That causes air to be sucked into the nose and mouth.

While many people know that movement of the diaphragm is essential for breathing, almost nobody understands how the diaphragm actually moves.

The diaphragm is a large, internal muscle which runs in a bell shape under the rib cage. It divides the trunk of the body into two sections. When the diaphragm lowers, the lungs have more room to expand.

Contrary to popular belief, however, the diaphragm does not expand and contract. It is a smooth muscle like the extensor muscles of the back, not a striated muscle like the biceps. It has little ability to move itself.

The diaphragm is actually moved by a series of muscles which are anchored in the lower back, just above the pelvis. They connect with the third, fourth, and fifth lumbar vertebrae. When we breathe automatically, these muscles pull the diaphragm down. These muscles are so "unconscious" that few people even know they exist.

When I explained this to the class, Tom was fascinated.

"Do you think we could learn to control them?" he asked.

"We probably could learn to influence them through biofeedback," I replied, "but that isn't necessary. How many of you have seen a baby breathe?"

June, Storm, and Bill raised their hands.

"What happens?" I asked.

"I remember my daughter's abdomen used to swell up like a balloon," June said. "I was always amazed. It seemed so effortless. Like she was just filling with air."

"She was," I replied. "What about her pelvis—did you notice anything there?"

"I can't remember. Wait, didn't it used to rock?"

"Exactly. When a baby breathes, his abdomen expands like a balloon and his pelvis rocks gently with every breath. The breathing muscles which I have just discussed actually cause the pelvis to rock, affecting many other muscles. It is this chain reaction which causes the abdomen to expand during breathing. In fact, though the air only goes as far down as the lungs, muscles stretch and contract all the way down the legs with every breath, creating a feeling of a full breath going all the way down the legs."

"I know what you mean," said Duke. "I get that feeling sometimes when I'm doing Yogic breathing."

"Well, I've never had that feeling in my life," said Bill. "Look, when I breathe, my abdomen doesn't expand at all. Just my chest." He illustrated.

"Me too," said Storm. "What does it mean when you only breathe in your chest?"

"There is a whole other portion of the breathing apparatus which I haven't talked about yet: the rib cage. Each rib can move in three different ways—away from the spine in back, away from the breastbone in front, and away from each other. While the movement of the ribs does not give as much space to the lungs as the movement of the diaphragm, it serves as an important aspect of breathing. You and Bill have cut off from the larger half of your breathing apparatus. As of now, you're only taking partial breaths."

"That's terrible," Storm said. "I don't want to breathe only halfway. I want to breathe completely."

"Believe me, you're not alone," I responded. "Especially with the American tight jeans syndrome."

Lisa, who had been listening on and off, perked up. "What's that?" she asked.

"People wear tight jeans to look good," I replied. "But they lose the lower half of their breathing apparatus. They make a good impression, they look sexy, but they can't breathe. It's a perfect example of making 'how it looks' more important than 'how it feels.' "

Lisa, who liked to show off her attractive figure in tight designer jeans, was nonplussed. "I'll wear something looser next time," she muttered.

"It would probably make the exercises much easier." I turned back to Storm. "Most people breathe primarily in either the chest or the abdomen. There are very few adults who have anything like the range of breathing of the average baby.

"Like the movement of the diaphragm, the movement of the ribs causes a chain reaction of muscle extensions and contractions, this time into the shoulders and neck and down the arms. It would not be an exaggeration to say that *a full breath involves almost every muscle in the body. Any tension which constricts any muscle in your body is also interfering with your breathing.*"

EXERCISES

Don't skip this section! Whenever I read books of this kind, I always skip the exercises, intending to come back to them. I rarely do. For this reason I have made the exercises as simple as possible. If you are reading through the book,

I suggest you read through the exercises slowly and at least do them in your mind. Your experience of these exercises will help you better assimilate the knowledge you may have gained from the first part of this chapter. If you are the type who likes to "get right down to it," go right ahead. However: *Don't push or force yourself. Do only what feels comfortable.*

Breath Awareness

Notice yourself right now. Are you breathing? If not, breathe. There are many guidelines I will be giving you in this work, but there is only one rule: *Breathe.* Or, more precisely, stop holding your breath and allow yourself to breathe.

Notice how you are breathing. Where does the air come in? Your nose? Your mouth? How far does it go down? Do you feel your chest move? Your stomach?

Don't try to change anything. Just observe.

Lie down on your back on a fairly hard surface (a carpeted floor is ideal) and pay attention to your breathing. Is it easier to breathe lying down? How does your breathing change? Where do you notice movement in your body? Stay on the floor for five or ten minutes and notice what happens. Check your body and see how the breath affects each part of it.

Bend your knees one at a time and bring

them up toward the ceiling so that the soles of your feet are flat on the floor. Does this change your breathing?

Try a simple movement: roll your head a little bit from side to side. Do you breathe during the movement or does your breathing suddenly stop? Continue to roll your head. Does your breathing change in any way? Stop the movement and notice whether your breathing is still the same.

Leave your head in the center and let your legs down one at a time. Again, notice how your breathing changes.

You can do this exercise as long as you like. But if it starts to get at all painful or boring, or when you have had enough, roll gently to a sitting position, still noticing your breath. If you are working with a friend, you can share what you observe with him or her.

Taking It Further

Observe your breathing in different situations. How do you breathe when you're relaxed? When you're excited? When you're talking to a friend? A business associate? A lover? Your boss?

Are there times when you stop breathing? Notice them and remind yourself to breathe.

How do you feel when you don't breathe? When you do?

For the next few weeks, at least several times

a day, notice your breathing. As we continue these exercises and your breathing begins to change, notice that also.

As you continue these exercises, you will be amazed to discover the radical positive effect simple awareness can have on your breathing.

RESULTS

As my students lay on the floor, monitoring their breathing, June began to yawn. Each time she yawned, she would stifle it, putting her hand demurely over her mouth. She opened her eyes and looked around to make sure nobody saw. I told her to let herself yawn if she wanted to.

In a few minutes, Tom was yawning also. He yawned noisily and didn't cover his mouth. Within a few minutes, everyone in the class, including myself, was yawning.

Yawning feels so good that when we sense someone else yawning, our bodies want to yawn, too. The yawn is the quickest way for our bodies to get a "hit" of oxygen and get rid of carbon dioxide. Yawning also stretches the face and chest muscles and brings tears to wash out the eyes. It is one of the best things our bodies can do for themselves. So of course our society prohibits it.

I encourage you to yawn as often as possible. The only rules about yawning in my class

are that you can't cover your mouth and you
have to make as much noise as possible.

At the beginning of the next class, the students reported on what they had noticed during the week:

"I was amazed at how many times I caught
myself holding my breath," said Tom.

"I noticed that, also," said June. "Any time
I have to do something, I stop breathing."

"I was amazed at how much my breathing
changed at different times," said Storm. "Whenever I got excited, I started to hyperventilate.
And my voice got high, too."

"I don't know if it relates to the class," June
said, "but I slept really well that night. I had
a lot of dreams. They were more vivid than
usual."

"I felt real energetic after class. I couldn't
get to sleep," said Duke. "And it was like that
the whole next day."

"I didn't notice anything at all," said Bill.

"What about you, Lisa?" I asked.

"I seemed a little nervous all week. I guess
it couldn't relate to the class."

"It could," I responded. *"When your breathing begins to change, everything else begins to change
also."*

3

THE PERFECT BODY

We tend to be so fascinated by the workings and power of our minds that we often view our bodies as obstacles to be overcome. Yet the human body is truly one of the wonders of nature. Not as strong or as fast as many other animals, without claws or fur to protect us, we are still the most physically adaptable of all animals, with tremendous flexibility and endurance.

Your body is not only perfectly designed to serve you, it is also an integral part of who you are. Your body is constantly trying to tell you what it wants, what will make it happy and comfortable. Your skeleton is designed to support you without chronic muscular tension or any trace of lower back pain—if you can only learn to let it.

A healthy working relationship with your own body is the second step to personal power. This chapter is the beginning of the end for stiff necks, flabby muscles, weak backs, headaches, etc.

Instead of trying to beat your body into submission, you need to learn to listen to it, trust it, and free it from tension. As you liberate your body from restrictions, you become the leader in an exciting partnership which gets you where you want to go. You will find yourself becoming more expressive and living more expansively.

Good Posture

My talk about the perfect human body produced considerable skepticism among my students.

"When my back starts hurting," Bill began, "my body doesn't seem so all-fired perfect to me."

"I get back pain too," June said. "Once I was laid up with it for three months."

"Low back pain is indeed endemic to our culture," I responded. "It even made the cover of *Time* magazine recently. Many doctors and other experts see lower back pain as evidence of some sort of inherent flaw in the human body. If that were so, there wouldn't be so many cultures in which low back pain is not a problem."

"Are there?" said Bill.

"Indeed there are. Low back pain is largely a creation of American 'comfort.' We don't use our backs properly and they pay us back. Chairs are among the main villains. Sitting on your heels like the Japanese do, or sitting cross-legged like the Indians, or 'hunkering down' like peasants in many countries—all of these ways of sitting stretch and balance back muscles and promote proper breathing. Slouching down into a comfortable chair tends to produce muscle collapse.

"There is no inherent flaw in human anatomy. *We are perfectly designed to stand fully erect and we are the only animal able to do so.*"

"I know that I tend to slouch," said Duke. "It feels comfortable, but I know it can't be good for me."

This was indeed true. Duke had a severe slouch. One that would cause him trouble in years ahead if nothing was done about it.

"What would it mean to you to stand up straight?" I asked.

Duke assumed a military posture: head up, chin out, shoulders back, stomach in. He looked considerably taller.

"Is that good posture?" I asked.

"That's the way I try to stand, when I think about it," said Tom.

"He looks a lot taller," put in Storm.

I could see the rest of the class also trying to stand or sit up straight.

"Are you comfortable?" I asked.

"It feels lousy," Duke admitted.

"What about breathing?" I asked. "Are you still breathing?"

"Not very much."

"The problem is that you are trying to consciously correct an unconscious process. When you try to control your body, to impose a set of rules on it, it's almost inevitable that you will become tense and stop breathing."

With some relief, everybody gave up their attempts at "good posture" and relaxed.

"Is it better to slouch?" June asked.

"For Duke at this point, absolutely. Correcting his slouch has to be done in a completely different way than forcing him to stand up straight. Good posture does not require effort or strain. It is always comfortable and promotes full breathing.

"You see," I went on, "there are a lot of rules for good posture and breathing. *All of them are wrong*. They are all attempts to impose a conscious control of the body, which is perfectly designed to do all of these things itself. And the body is designed with a wide range of possible responses to meet a variety of situations. We are too flexible to have hard-and-fast rules.

"If you watch a baby, he is constantly experimenting, trying out different movements. He has no one telling him whether he is right or wrong. He moves for two reasons. One, if it is useful to achieve some end. Two, for the sheer joy of it."

"You keep talking about babies," Bill said. "But we're not babies any more. Babies crawl, they don't even stand up yet. I stand up straight. My father taught me to stand up straight and

I learned." Bill did indeed have a "military posture." He held himself stiffly erect, sucking in his stomach. "Babies don't need rules. Adults do."

"You don't look comfortable, standing like that," observed Storm.

"I'm comfortable enough," Bill replied.

How We Learn

"You are right about one thing, Bill," I put in. "Adults are always seeking out rules. There are countless experts on how to breathe, stand, eat, and live, and most of them disagree. I'm sure you'd all like rules from me. And when I get careless, I give them to you."

"But we're here to learn," said Tom. "We've got to be learning *something*."

"We do the greatest amount of our learning from birth to about the age of five. We learn to walk and talk, to behave and relate to others. And we do it all without being taught. We learn through imitation, discovery, and experiment. That is the kind of learning I am trying to provide for you, learning which actually changes you, which rearranges the neural pathways in your brain. I'm not just trying to provide you with information, I'm trying to help you change and grow."

"I still don't understand," said Bill. "How can we change and grow without rules, at least some sort of rules? If we're standing or breathing *wrong,* you have to show us how to do it *right.*"

"I can't show you how to do it right, because there isn't a right; there's only what's best for you . . . We are going to be working to reeducate our kinesthetic sensibilities, our sense of our own bodies and their position in space. We will be doing exercises derived from the work of Moshe Feldenkrais.

"Moshe Feldenkrais was both a good scientist and a European judo champion. When he injured his knees playing soccer and the doctors offered him no hope of a cure, he set about retraining himself. He developed a series of repetitions and combinations of small simple movements, which are done for their own sake. There is no goal of achievement, no pushing oneself. The movements are done by both the body and the mind, and they are done one side at a time.

"Feldenkrais's goal is to reeducate the nervous system, breaking habitual patterns of movement and mind sets. By trying and expecting difficulty, we get in our own way. Feldenkrais teaches us to allow the movement to happen and to observe. We learn to go by how a movement feels rather than by what we think it should be."

"What kind of movements does Feldenkrais have you do?" asked Tom.

"We'll be doing an exercise derived from this system a little later," I replied. "But let me tell you a story which will give you an idea.

"I was sitting in a restaurant with a friend of mine who is a Feldenkrais's practitioner watching a baby who was sitting on the next table. The baby had hold of its toes and was swinging its foot gently and rhythmically back and forth. 'Isn't that cute,' my friend said, 'he's doing a Feldenkrais exercise.' "

"So we're going to be moving around like babies," said Bill. "I still don't see what it's going to do for us."

The Primitive Brain

"Let me try to explain in terms of the human brain and how it works. There are three parts to the brain. Does anybody know what they are?"

"There's the left brain and the right brain," responded Duke. "The left brain is the logical part and the right brain is the creative part."

"Exactly," I replied. "The left brain is the logical, rational, figuring, planning part of the brain. It thinks in words and analyzes. The left brain—actually the left forebrain—is the blessing and curse of our civilization.

"The right brain is creative and intuitive. It thinks in wholes and images. The left brain might look at a tree in terms of how tall it is, what kind it is, and how many board-feet of lumber it contains. The right brain might look at the same tree and go 'Aaah, how beautiful.' "

"Is that the part of the brain we're trying to develop in this class?" asked Tom.

"There has been much written and taught about the function of the right brain in recent years and its usefulness as a balance to Americans' unchecked use of the left brain," I responded. "However, in this class I am most concerned with a third part of the brain, one we haven't mentioned yet. This is the automatic, primitive part of the brain which we share with all animals. It controls the basic functions of breathing, regulating the internal organs, relating to gravity, and so forth. We can call it the 'hindbrain.'

"Our hindbrains are proportionately the same size as the hindbrains of other animals. As we go up the evolutionary scale, however, the left and right forebrains increase dramatically in size (as Carl Sagan points out in his book *The Dragons of Eden*). In humans, the left and right forebrains are enormous, proportionately much larger than those of any other animal (except the dolphin).

"Because the left forebrain is so large and so worshiped by our society, it keeps looking around for more work to do. It is like a huge government agency, creating unnecessary regulations. The left brain gets involved in posture, breathing, et cetera—processes which it can only distort. *The first stage of our work together is to get the left brain out of the way so that the hindbrain can do its job.*"

"It still doesn't sound right," Bill commented. "It sounds like you're asking us to become unconscious."

"Let me put it this way," I responded. "It's a lot easier to ride a horse than to pull it. *We can harness the power of the hindbrain by observing and gently guiding its functions rather than jumping in with both feet and trying to take over.* Unfortunately, most exercise systems and rules of posture try to force the body and are thus self-defeating."

Yielding to Gravity

"Let me give you an example Feldenkrais uses in his book *The Body and Mature Behavior.* How many of you have seen a rodeo or a cowboy movie where a cowboy throws a steer? What happens? How do you throw a steer?"

"You grab it by the horns and turn its head," Tom responded immediately.

"Do you turn its head quickly or slowly?"

"Quickly," said Tom. "Otherwise the steer won't go down and you'll have one angry steer on your hands."

"You have to jerk the head quickly and sharply until the horns are perpendicular to the ground," I added. "Then *the body follows the head* and the steer thumps to the ground. How about in cowboy movies where a horse falls down and then gets up again? How does he do it?"

Tom responded again. "He gets up in two stages. His head rights itself. Then his body follows."

"Exactly. All animals have a mechanism in the inner ear which orients them to gravity. Their 'posture' is determined by this mechanism, which is automatically controlled in the hindbrain. Only primates have a manual override. Primates can control their relationship to gravity by what they see, rather than what they feel."

"What's wrong with that?" asked June.

"Nothing's wrong with it. Except that people tend to figure out how they think they should stand and move, rather than trusting their built-in mechanism, their kinesthetic sense."

"You're talking apples and oranges again," said Bill. "First it was grown-ups and babies, now it's man and four-legged animals. Walking on only two legs has got to be more complicated."

"Thank you for bringing that up, Bill," I responded. "That gets me right back to man's fully erect posture. Man's only inborn fear is the fear of falling. In our society, especially, we have developed the notion that we have to hold ourselves up or we will lose our balance and fall down. This is the same kind of unconscious, deep-seated, and totally groundless fear as the fear that if we don't make sure to breathe, we will die. In fact, our bodies are perfectly designed to hold us up with a minimum of effort. Our skeleton and muscles can channel our weight through two legs with ease and elegance."

"What do you mean, we try to hold ourselves up?" asked Duke.

"It's time for my talk on the human skeleton," I responded.

The Human Skeleton

The body is designed so that the bones of the skeleton are stacked one on top of another. To maintain this arrangement, the muscles of the body need a very small amount of tension, what is called "tonus."

Most of us tense our muscles much more than we need to. We are literally holding ourselves up with our shoulders and chests rather than allowing these parts to yield to gravity and letting the bones support each other.

The skull is balanced precariously on top of the spine. In laboratory skeletons, the skull has to be wired into place. Otherwise, it will fall off. The arms also have to be wired. The entire shoulder girdle has only one bony connection to the torso: the collarbone joins the breastbone just above the first ribs.

In other words, your head is meant to be literally 'above it all,' only loosely connected with the rest of your body. It is free to seek the upright position, responding to signals from your inner ear. Your shoulder girdle is designed to float, with your arms hanging freely at your sides, yielding to gravity. The arms and hands are free to reach out and act on the world— one of the main reasons for man's incredible achievements.

Now, look at the chest. Most people think of the ribs as being the same height in front and in back. In fact, the ribs are much lower in the front of the body than where they connect with the spine. They, too, are yielding to gravity. Like the head and shoulders and arms, the chest has nothing to do with keeping the body upright.

Your body is kept upright by your spine, pelvis, and legs. It's important to remember that the spine is not a solid column, but twenty-two separate vertebrae stacked on top of each other. Each vertebra floats on a cushion of spinal fluid. In a skeleton, it looks as if the spine is a solid mass because the spinal fluid dries up after death.

As you look down the vertebrae of the spine, you will see that they get larger. That is because they have to carry increasingly more weight. The lumbar, or lower back, vertebrae are actually so large as to extend almost halfway into the lower abdomen.

Now, the weight from the spine must be transferred through the pelvis down the legs. This is where the system frequently breaks down. Most people have pelvises which are locked in one position, either tilted forward or back. The former is most common and causes a sway back.

To illustrate this point to my students, I tilted my pelvis forward, stuck my head out, and walked around the room. Most people practice some variation of that walk. The opposite tilt of the pelvis, which is less common, produces what I call the "John Wayne look." To illustrate this, I stuck my hands in my back pockets, tilted by pelvis back, let my groin thrust forward, and swaggered around the room. This time there was general snickering. My students recognized the macho, "look what I've got" walk, common to certain men and some women also. Most of us, however, have the opposite tendency and keep the genitals as hidden and protected as possible.

Neither of these positions is "wrong." The problem is that the pelvis is designed to move constantly, to sit directly under the spine no matter what movements we make. A pelvis that is locked, fixed in place, leads to lower back pain. Weight doesn't transfer properly from the lower vertebrae, through the pelvis, and down the legs. We begin to compensate by holding ourselves up with muscles in the chest, neck and shoulders, sacrificing the freedom which nature gave us.

There is a strong connection between the transfer of weight we've just been talking about and the breathing process we talked about in the last chapter. The muscles which control the diaphragm are located in the lower back, at the third, fourth, and fifth lumbar vertebrae. If those vertebrae are interfered with, the breathing muscles actually get involved in the process of holding us up. They are not free to pull the diaphragm. So you can see how posture and breathing are interrelated. If you improve your posture, you improve your breathing, and vice versa.

In the last chapter, I talked about how a baby's pelvis rocks every time it breathes. A full breath causes a rocking of the pelvis. If the pelvic muscles are tense, the pelvis can't rock, and breathing is restricted.

The Jaw

There is one part of the skeleton which we have not explored yet and which has considerable influence on our breathing: the jaw. The jaw is connected to the rest of the skull by a hinge; two small bones protrude from the back of the jaw and fit into holes in the skull. If you want to feel this hinge, put your fingers in your ears and move your jaw.

On a skeleton, the jaw has to be wired to stay in place. It is designed to yield to gravity and drop from the skull. When we are alive, however, the jaw is attached to the rest of the skull by two of the strongest muscles in the body. If you want to feel these muscles, put your fingers below your cheeks and back toward your ears and press. When I told the class to try this, the results were striking.

"Ow," Tom burst out.

"You've got it," I said.

"It really hurts."

"That's because the muscles are tight. In all the time I've been teaching, I've only had two students whose jaw muscles were loose enough so they didn't hurt when they were pressed."

"Mine don't hurt," put in Storm.

"Then you're probably pressing in the wrong place." I went over to her and pressed my fingers in further back toward her ears. Her face immediately tensed up in pain.

"I see what you mean," she said.

With morbid curiosity, each person found his jaw muscles and produced the pain.

"These muscles are so tight," I went on, "because they are among the strongest muscles in our body. Our jaws were designed for biting and tearing. Our jaw muscles are strong enough to bite through someone's arm." June and Bill gasped.

"If anyone has seen the movie *The Boys from Brazil*, Gregory Peck and Laurence Olivier get into such a violent fight that they actually bite each other.

"In our society, the jaw muscles are under-utilized. We tend to hold our jaws tightly shut. We are a tight-lipped and tight-jawed society. However, if our jaw muscles are relaxed, the jaw will hang open slightly."

"Won't that make you look stupid?" asked June.

"No. We have a fear of a jaw slack making us look stupid, but that's based on a misconception. There is a certain form of idiocy in which the jaw muscles lose all tonus and the jaw just hangs open."

"You mean, like this?" Tom asked. He let his mouth drop open and deliberately looked dumb. Everyone laughed.

"Yes, that's what people are afraid of. In fact, if you let the jaw drop open, no one will see. The opening is covered by the lips. My jaw is always slightly open, but it's not noticeable."

"You mean, like this?" Bill asked. He held his mouth wide open.

"You're holding your mouth open. I'm talking about letting go of the jaw muscles just enough to allow the jaw to drop open. It's a small change. The jaw actually drops slightly down and slightly back toward your neck."

I demonstrated on Tom, moving his jaw slightly back and down.

"Hey, I feel like I'm getting more air," he said.

"You are. That's why letting the jaw go is so important. A tight jaw keeps us from getting an adequate supply of air. It is one of the body's great defenses against breathing. A tight jaw is a sign of stubbornness because if you don't breathe, you can't change. You can defeat any form of therapy, psychological or physical, just by keeping a tight jaw."

Body Language

"If locking our jaws is self-defeating, why do we do it?" asked June.

"That's a very good question," I replied. "Why do we defeat ourselves? I was talking last class about Wilhelm Reich. Reich worked not only on increasing the breathing, but also on poking into tight muscles to release the emotions held there. He believed that *in order to avoid feeling or expressing anything unpleasant, we not only restrict our breathing, we also tighten our muscles.* He called this tightening 'armoring' because he felt it was like putting on a suit of armor.

"Reich believed that a person's character, or personality, could be determined by observing his body. In this, he was completely in agreement with folk wisdom. People talk about a 'determined chin.' A severely jutting jaw can be a sign of tremendous defiance and aggressiveness—Mussolini is, perhaps, an extreme example of this. On the other hand, a receding chin is often taken as a sign of weakness or lack of determination.

"Along with the jaw, a raised chest can be seen as aggressive, a sign of inflated self-esteem. A collapsed chest is a sign of a lack of pride. Other typical body language includes raised shoulders protecting the neck and indicating fear. I call this the 'Turtle Complex' or 'if you don't stick your neck out, you won't get it cut off.' There are many, many other examples.

"Before I began this work, my own chest was raised slightly but firmly. I was proud, but I didn't want it to show."

"What's wrong with being proud?" asked Bill. "I'm proud."

"There's nothing wrong with being proud. *The problem comes when you're locked into one position, physically or emotionally.*"

"And this work can help us change that?" asked Duke.

"Absolutely."

"I'm still not sure I understand why we lock our jaws," June put in.

"We are holding back feelings of rage, which are unacceptable in our society. We are a tight-jawed society. We are also a tight-assed society—the ass being one of the other places in the body where rage is held."

Storm and Lisa tittered.

"I'm serious," I went on. "One of the amazing things about body metaphors is that they are often literally true. If you say someone gives you a pain in the neck, he probably does."

"You mean that someone can literally give you a pain in the neck?" asked Tom.

"They sure can. If you're upset with someone and you don't want to express it, you can tense all the muscles in your neck to keep you from saying anything."

"That sounds familiar," said June. "You were saying earlier that we tend to lock our pelvises. Is that related to locking our jaws?"

"To some extent," I responded. "The pelvis and the jaw are closely related in a way I will talk about later. And both the jaw and the ass tighten up to hold in rage.

"But there are other factors involved in locking the pelvis. First, the kind of toilet training we receive, and when we receive it, can influence us for life. When we are toilet trained too young, our sphincter control has not been developed and we have to tighten much larger muscles that are actually designed to hold us up. Once we have done this, we tend to keep these muscles tightened for fear of 'losing control.' Secondly, of course, we are afraid to move our pelvises because we have been brought up with a great deal of sexual repression."

"Will this work cure sexual repression?" asked Lisa, expressing the most interest she had shown thus far.

"Let me put it this way," I replied. "It will certainly get your body moving again."

EXERCISES

Again, *do not skip this section.* If you are reading through the book, read through this exercise slowly and do it in your mind. Then, do it, experiencing the changes in your body.

On a physical level, the movements I'm going to be describing are ridiculously easy. They are all done lying on the floor and involve the simplest possible movements of shoulders, hips, feet, neck, and pelvis. Most people find them relaxing and pleasurable—a form of body meditation, which gives the overworked left brain a rest from worrying and planning. However, they do call for considerable concentration and they can prove frustrating for some. They can also be upsetting, as they can make you aware of physical tension you didn't know you had.

Again, *don't push or force yourself. Do only what feels comfortable.*

Body Awareness

The following exercise is derived from my interpretation of the work of Moshe Feldenkrais. Feldenkrais's work hinges on two remarkably simple, yet profound discoveries:

1) In order to learn, we must involve both mind and body; mindless repetition of movements teaches us nothing. To learn, we must move with awareness of what is happening.

2) *The body learns one side at a time.* This relates to the fact that the left forebrain controls the right side of the body, while the right forebrain controls the left side. When one side of the body learns something, it can teach the other side.

The simple movements which we will be combining are completely different from push-ups or sit-ups in that they involve no strength. They are about relaxing and loosening rather than tensing and "building yourself up." They differ from Yoga in that they involve small movements rather than holding positions.

All movements should be small and easy. There is no one to impress. No one has to see how far you are moving so don't move very far. At first you may not be able to feel any movement unless you exaggerate it, but as you continue, your kinesthetic sense will improve. All you need is enough movement to know that you have made a movement.

Rather than size and accomplishment, go for grace, continuity, and ease.

If the movement is jerky, make it smaller.

Take your time.

The exercise, though nonstrenuous, is still meant to be done with plenty of pauses for rest. Don't think of these as repetitions; think of each movement as a complete whole, involving a beginning, a middle, and an end. Take a little rest after each movement. Model your movements after the involuntary movements of the body which are controlled by the hind-brain. For every second the heart works, it rests for more than a second. In this way, it can go on for years and years. Move as if you are going to be doing these movements for a long time. I can, myself, spend hours on the floor, meditating and enjoying my way through an exercise.

The rest between movements is as important as the movements themselves.

You may find yourself getting sleepy as you do this exercise and possibly dozing off. That is fine. Change can occur most comfortably in that border area between waking and sleeping in which everyday worries and left-brain concerns are given a rest. This is the area which hypnosis utilizes, and I have more than once been accused of practicing hypnosis—mostly by hypnotists—when I give these exercises. While it is not necessary that you enter this state, it is a possibility that can be welcomed.

It is often a problem doing exercises from a book, especially as these are all done lying on the floor. It is difficult to remain fully relaxed while you read the next direction. Accordingly, I suggest you either have your partner read the exercise to you or put the exercise on tape. If neither alternative is possible, you can try reading the exercise several times, then doing what you remember.

The following exercise runs several printed pages. I could have written it out as follows:

Lie down on the floor.

1) Lift left shoulder toward the ceiling (25 times)
2) Extend right heel (25 times)
3) Alternate the two movements (25 times)

Obviously, this would have been a lot shorter.

But it would have missed the whole point. During the exercise, I want to focus your attention on different parts of your body. I want to keep your mind an active participant in the work. I use language carefully to help you avoid any straining or trying, and, hopefully, to make the whole process interesting, not merely a bunch of boring repetitions of the same movement. Finally, I want to call your attention to how your whole body is affected when you move any part of it.

With that long but essential introduction, here is the exercise.

Shoulder and Heel

Lie down on the floor on a thick carpet and/ or a foam pad. (A bed does not give you enough support.) Notice how your body connects with the ground, which parts touch and which parts don't. Notice the small of your back. How far off the ground is it? You can check this externally with your hand. You can also tell internally. Notice the way things really are without trying to "correct" them to what you think *I* think is "right." Learn to accept yourself as you are now.

Are both arms lying the same way? If not, how do they differ? The same with your legs. Is your spine straight? Begin to notice the differences between the right and left side. Notice your ribs on each side, your shoulders, the small of your back. Are they the same or different?

How about your breathing? Are you breathing? If not, breathe. How are you breathing? Where does the air come in and where does it go? Is it the same on both sides or does one lung feel bigger?

Now, begin to roll your head very gently from side to side. Is one side easier? Is the pathway different on the right than on the left? Do this several times, then stop and observe. Has anything changed, particularly in the small of your back?

Now, feel that you have a string attached to your left shoulder. The string reaches up to the ceiling. Someone on the ceiling is going to pull the string gently up, and your shoulder will move up toward the ceiling slightly; then he's going to release the string, and your shoulder will float gently down.

Keep allowing this movement. Your shoulder goes up gently, then returns gently to place. Don't worry about how far you go. The movement can be very small. Just allow it to be as smooth and graceful and flowing as possible. As you continue the movement, notice your breathing. (Make sure that you are still breathing.) When do you like to breathe in and when do you breathe out? Do you breathe in as the shoulder comes up and out as the shoulder goes down? Or vice versa?

Try reversing your breathing. See how that feels. Then return to whichever breathing is more comfortable.

Notice any other changes in your body as a result of just moving your shoulder. What's happening in your ribs? Your back? Does your head feel like moving?

Now, let the movement get smaller and smaller, until no one looking at you can see you are doing anything. It's just your little secret. . . . Then, let it get even smaller until it's only a thought in your mind. . . . Then, let it disappear completely.

Now, scan your body and see if anything has changed. Compare your left shoulder with your right shoulder. Are they different? Does one feel lighter? Heavier? Bigger? Warmer? Compare your left arm with your right arm. The left side of your ribs with your right. Notice the differences. Does one side of the small of your back seem closer to the ground than the other? How about your legs? Any difference there?

Roll your head from side to side. Does one way feel like you're rolling uphill? Is one way much easier? How about your breathing? Do you feel like you're getting more breath on one side?

What about your body as a whole? Do you feel any differently? Any longer? Or lighter? Getting more air in?

The changes you are feeling come after only a very few minutes of the simplest possible exercise.

Now, let's try something else. Imagine that you have a golf ball which is resting against the sole of your right foot. You are going to move the golf ball slightly by extending your right heel to push it gently away. Then let the heel go back into place.

As you continue to do this, slowly and gently, pushing and releasing, notice how the movement extends from your foot. What happens to your ankle? In your calf muscle? What happens in your knee? Does it move toward the floor as you push with your heel?

Continue the motion. What happens in your thigh? In your hip joint and pelvis?

What about your breathing? When do you like to breathe in and when do you breathe out? Continue the movement and continue to notice its repercussions.

Now, let the movement get smaller and smaller until no one can see you doing it. Then let it be a thought in your mind. Then let go of it entirely and rest.

Now, scan your body again, comparing the right side with the left side, and notice the changes. Roll your head from side to side again, and notice if that has changed. Rest.

Now, try the first movement, letting your left shoulder rise gently a little bit toward the ceiling and then letting it go. Has that changed at all? Has it become any easier?

Try alternating the two movements, letting the left shoulder rise and fall and letting the right heel extend and release. Can you feel a connection between them? Draw an imaginary line from your right heel to your left shoulder. Where does it cross the spine?

Get a sense of how your whole body participated in this simple alternation. Let the movement get progressively smaller, and rest.

Notice your body. How does your spine feel? Is it straight or does it seem to curve to one side? How about your ribs? Compare your left and right sides again. Has the difference between them increased or diminished? Check your breathing. Does it seem to be filling more of your body than it did when you first lay down?

Try the movement of raising your shoulder one more time. How does it compare to when you first lay down? Roll your head easily from side to side again. How does that compare?

Roll to the side and come up easily to a standing position, using your arms and legs to help you and using your head as little as possible.

How do you feel? What do you notice? Are the changes you noticed lying down the same as when you stand up? Do your two legs feel different? Your arms?

Take a few gentle steps and notice how it feels to walk. Do you use your body differently from usual? What are the differences? How does your body behave in the gravitational field?

Look into a mirror and observe yourself, especially your face. See if it looks different.

Have your cheeks dropped? Your lips? Are your eyes brighter? How does your body look?

When you do this exercise again, add rolling your head to the other two movements. Try rolling your head easily to the right as your left shoulder lifts slightly. See if you can correlate the two movements so that head and shoulder move at the same time. Then let your head roll to the left as your right heel extends. You can experiment to see which way is the most comfortable for your head to roll. You may well find that allowing your head to roll makes the whole movement easier.

Taking It Further

During the course of the week, observe how you move. Notice when there is unnecessary tension in your movements. Do you tighten up your face when you walk or when you type? You do not necessarily need to let go of the tension. Just notice it. You will find your body letting go all by itself.

Notice how bodily tension correlates with holding your breath. See if you can let tension go just by allowing yourself to breathe. See if you can feel that certain movements and postures promote free breathing.

Notice other people. See how and where they hold tension. Observe their body language. What are their bodies saying? Perhaps their body message is very different from their words.

Do this homework easily and enjoyably, without becoming obsessed with it. Only observe as long as it is fun. Perhaps you can put in two periods of ten minutes a day observing, then slip back into blissful ignorance. Do not use this knowledge to judge other people or yourself. Merely expand your awareness. Remember, awareness without judgment is the first step to change.

RESULTS

My students slowly got to their feet and began to move around the room.

"We look like *The Night of the Living Dead,*" said Tom.

"I feel relaxed. I mean, really relaxed," said Storm. "I don't remember when I've ever felt so relaxed."

"I feel relaxed and yet full of energy," said June. "And my arms seem to be just hanging at my sides."

The class stood in a circle and looked at each other. I went over to June and lifted one arm. When I let go, it flopped easily back to her side.

"It's like my arms are just hanging there," June continued. "I don't feel like there's something I should be doing with them."

"That's what the arms are supposed to do," I said. "Hang in there until they are needed.

Remember our discussion of the shoulder girdle."

"My hands are tingling," said Lisa. "Are they supposed to do that?"

"They are for you."

"I don't like it." She began to shake her hands out, trying to get rid of the tingling.

"If you can, try to just leave it alone. It will go away in a while. Is anyone else getting tingling?"

"I am," said Tom. "I'm getting tingling all over. It's really a killer."

"What does 'killer' mean?" Bill asked.

"Great," Tom translated. "It's like my whole body's alive with energy. It's just buzzing all over. I feel like I could zap someone with it."

"Go ahead," I said.

Tom pointed his fingers at Bill and "zapped" him. "Did you feel that?" he asked.

"Feel what?" asked Bill.

"I think I'm getting some tingles, too," said Storm. "Mostly in my legs. It feels almost like my legs are asleep. What is it?"

"Tom was exactly right. You are actually feeling energy flowing in your body. It's one of the purposes of this work, to increase your energy flow. We'll be talking about it in a few weeks."

"I don't like it," Lisa repeated.

"What else does anyone notice?"

"I feel really planted," said June. "Like I'm standing really firmly on both feet."

"If you look around, you'll see something you won't see at any cocktail party. Everyone has both feet firmly on the floor. With just a few minutes of doing this exercise, you will find your body equally balanced on both legs, the way nature intended it to be."

"I keep swaying from front to back," said Storm. "I feel like I'm going to fall over."

"Your body is just experimenting with balance. That's why I tell people to get up very slowly. Otherwise you could fall right over."

"My left shoulder feels lower than my right," said Tom.

"It is. Quite a bit lower."

"Mine is, too," Storm put in. "I feel like I'm all crooked."

"I feel straighter than ever," said June. "I feel taller, too."

"I feel really light," said Storm. "Like I'm just floating."

"That's funny," said Tom. "I feel really heavy. Like I'm going to sink into the ground."

"The tingling stopped," said Lisa, with relief.

Duke, who had fallen asleep at the end of the exercise, was only now getting to his feet. Everyone stopped to watch him as his body slowly uncurled up. Without effort, he seemed to keep growing until he stood at his full height, looking down at the rest of us. At first I had thought Duke was about my height—five foot nine. When he forced himself to stand up straight, he looked about six feet. Now he stood at a graceful, effortless six foot four.

"I feel taller," he said.

There was a moment's silence. "Is he going to stay like that?" Tom asked.

"Not immediately, unfortunately. We can't undo years of habit with one new experience. But if he keeps doing the work, the change will become permanent."

"I really do feel taller," Duke repeated. "And I like it."

4

BORN TO ROAR: FREEING YOUR VOICE

We have been taught for so long to be reasonable, polite, and controlled that our voices have lost much of their range and power. And yet your voice is your most potent tool for reaching out and expressing yourself to others. Without an open channel of vocal expression, you cannot say what you mean or ask for what you want.

Freeing your voice is the third step to personal power. We are all born with vocal power—as evidenced by any baby when it starts to cry. We are all designed to make sound effortlessly, without strain. A full, free voice comes from the guts, not from the throat. As you drop habitual controls and allow things to happen, your voice will grow in richness and expression.

How the Voice Works

All of my students, like the majority of American adults, were holding back their vocal-expression. Duke was perhaps the most extreme. His voice was so breathy that it was very difficult to make out what he said.

Just as Duke slouched to hold back his physical power, so he spoke in a breathy manner to hold back his vocal power.

Storm had a different problem. While physically and verbally aggressive, she spoke in a little girl voice. On the telephone, callers were always mistaking her for her daughter.

"My therapist says that the problem with my voice is just psychological," Storm said. "I demand attention, but my voice keeps people from taking me seriously. Do you think that's true?"

"I think your therapist is pretty shrewd," I responded. "However, I don't believe that there is any such thing as 'just psychological.' *The mind and the body are one. Nowhere is this clearer than with the voice.* The voice is designed to express feelings, and using the voice is an assertive act. There is also a wonderful physiological mechanism involved. Both you and Duke could very profitably look at why you use your voices as you do. You also need to learn how to let go of the muscular tension that is constricting you."

"When will we do that?" Storm asked.

"We'll start right now," I responded. "Who knows how the voice works?"

"Well, there are vocal chords," put in Bill.

"Yeah, and the breath goes past them and they vibrate and that's how we speak," Tom finished.

"Is that it?" I asked.

"The vocal chords lengthen and shorten. That's how we get high and low sounds," added June.

"What you've said is partially accurate," I replied, "but it is misleading. You've put all the focus where most Americans put it: on the throat. However, when your voice tightens up, which part of you is usually constricted?"

"The throat," answered June.

"If you put all your attention on the throat, as your explanation suggests, what happens to it?"

"It tightens still more," Tom responded.

"Exactly. The first rule of voice production is that you have no throat. The sound comes from down in your guts, right out of your entire face, and there is nothing in between. Obviously, that is not physiologically accurate, but it is the most productive way to conceptualize making sound.

"Let me make the description a little more accurate. You spoke about vocal 'chords.' What do you think of when you think of a 'chord?'"

"Like a string," said June.

"Something thin and tight," put in Bill.

"The vocal chords are actually folds of skin," I continued, "tight enough as it is without an image that only adds tension.

"So to get back to your explanation, air comes up from the diaphragm, forced up by muscle changes that happen in the low back and the pelvis. The air goes through the vocal folds, which vibrate. That produces a sound like this. . . ." I made a sound like bones rattling deep in my throat.

"That sounds like a death rattle," said Tom.

"That's what happens when only the vocal folds vibrate. What else has to happen?"

"Well," said June, "we speak with the tongue and lips."

I made the sound again and moved my tongue and lips around. It was still a death rattle. "The tongue and lips only shape the sound once it's produced. There is a whole other process to producing it."

Everyone sat there, stumped. After a pause, I continued.

"You know the television commercial where a singer gets a glass to break by hitting a high note? How does that happen?"

Tom replied. "The high note gets the molecules in the glass to start vibrating. At a certain frequency, the glass can't hold together any more. It just shatters."

"Exactly. Sound is vibration. The singer's voice produces a secondary vibration in the glass. In the same way, the vibration of the vocal folds causes a secondary vibration in all the bones of the body, especially those of the face and chest. The voice we hear is made up of those secondary vibrations. The quality of sound depends on the number and range of the secondary vibrations produced.

"The general rule is very simple: *the more you vibrate, and the more widespread the vibrations throughout the body, the fuller and richer the sound.* When I speak after I've done some of the vocalizing work I'm going to show you, I can feel vibrations from the top of my skull to the soles of my feet."

"Are you saying that the more vibrations, the better the sound?" asked Bill.

"Not exactly. I'm talking about range of vibrations. I come from Brooklyn, and when I'm pressed I can do a pretty good Brooklyn accent," I said as I shifted into a strident dialect. "All I'm doing is putting all my vibrations right around my nose."

"Now," I dropped the accent, "I'm not stopping my nose from vibrating, but I'm allowing the rest of my face to vibrate also. That was an example of a highly nasal voice."

"It sure was," said Tom.

"Did you notice how loud it seemed? A lot of vibrations in one place makes your voice loud, but not rich. Vocal fullness comes from vibrating all over. Incidentally, what people sometimes call a nasal sound, like when you have a cold and your nose is congested, is actually de-nasal. Breath can't go out the nose, and because of the congestion the bones and cartilage can't vibrate."

"Sometimes when I have a cold, my voice drops," said June. "I just wish it would stay there."

"Your voice drops because you've stopped working so hard to constrict it. Many people have a deeper voice first thing in the morning for the same reason. In both cases, it takes too much energy to create all the neck tension we usually use to make sound. When the sound isn't interfered with, it comes out full and deep."

"I thought you were supposed to keep sound in your chest," said Tom. "Doesn't that give you a deeper sound?"

"It's a mistake to think of sound as limited to any one part of the body," I responded. "Deep sounds come from vibrations in the chest as well as the rest of the body. High sounds are produced in the head. *We are equipped to speak in a three-octave range. But most of us have vocal ranges of only half an octave.* Just as our breathing is designed to change in different situations, so are our voices. When I'm teaching, my voice tends to be concentrated in my chest, low and mellow. When I get excited, however," I said, demonstrating the change, "my voice will naturally rise way up into my head until I can feel the top of my skull vibrating." My altered voice, high and excited, filled the room.

"It doesn't sound so bad when you do it," said Storm. "Somehow, even though it's high, it still sounds full."

"That's because, even though my principal vibration is going up into my head, I am still vibrating throughout the rest of my body. The texture and richness of a voice comes from overtones and undertones. When I speak ordinarily, I am vibrating in my stomach and pelvis, an octave below my primary pitch, and in my forehead and the top of my skull, an octave above. When I get excited, my primary pitch moves upward, but I keep the undertones."

Masculine and Feminine: Emotion and the Voice

Every time we speak we commit an aggressive act. We fill the air with sound and we enter another's space. While we all have resistance around using our voices, the resistance is often shaped along sexual lines.

Women in our society are far more comfortable being vulnerable than powerful; this is reflected in their higher voices, with a preponderance of head tones. Even when they ask for what they want, women are trained to use a little girl voice—to plead and entreat, rather than demand. As a result, they often aren't taken seriously.

Many men have the opposite problem. They are brought up to be more comfortable expressing power, which relates to deep sounds. They are afraid of the vulnerability which high sounds express. Men are taught to demand, even when they might want to entreat or plead. They are taught to hide the vulnerable emotions of sadness or terror, to filter those emotions out of their sound. The result can be a tight, strained voice or an unnaturally low one, lacking the "feminine" head tones.

"I like having a low voice," put in Tom when I explained this to the class.

"You have a 'radio announcer' voice. It's deep and impressive, but it's not very expressive. It doesn't reveal anything about what you're feeling. The other most respected masculine sound in our society is the John Wayne–Clint Eastwood macho one, where teeth are clenched and so little sound gets out that we can hardly hear what they're saying, let alone get a clue as to what they're feeling."

"I guess that relates to my breathiness," ventured Duke. "I know I always have my teeth clenched." (This was indeed true.) "I grew up on the streets and I was a lot smarter and more studious than the kids I hung out with. It was a good idea not to show people how I felt. Maybe when I took the emotion out of my voice, I took the sound out of it, also."

"I don't want to reveal what I'm feeling," Tom replied. "Keep 'em guessing, that's my motto."

"That's right," Bill put in. "Who wants people to know what you're feeling? It could be dangerous. Especially in business."

"There are times, like in a business situation, when it may be better not to show your feelings. But there are times when you really need to show them. I'm trying to help you obtain that choice," I said.

"I think I show my feelings too much," said Storm. "When I'm angry, I really let people know it."

"You may tell people you're angry, but do you sound angry?" I replied. "Is the anger in your voice? Do your voice and expression convey what you're feeling?"

"I'm not sure."

"I have a sense that they don't. That's one of the things we'll be working on: to get your voice to express your power, so that it matches the rest of you better."

The Purpose of the Voice

Lisa had maintained her customary silence, but something was obviously bothering her. She had been fidgeting since the beginning of class and her expression was one of frustration.

"Lisa, you look like you want to say something," I said.

"I do. But it's hard for me. I always have trouble talking in groups. It's not so bad with friends."

She paused. We waited.

"I was just remembering a time, last year, when I walked in front of this crazy who was yelling at the cars on Sunset Boulevard. I guess I must have looked at him funny or something, but the next thing I knew, he grabbed me and started shaking me. And I couldn't scream. I just kept trying to get away and I couldn't even open my mouth. Finally, somebody must have seen what was happening because she yelled at the guy. He let me go and I walked away."

There was a silence.

"You've given up your most potent weapon," I said gently. "We've got to help you get it back."

"You should have kicked him the balls," said Storm.

"That might have worked," I agreed. "But screaming or calling for help is often more effective. Especially when there are people all around. It's the same principle as having a burglar alarm or a dog in your house.

"The voice is our greatest tool for connecting with other people. Before we start to use words, as babies, we make three basic sounds. When we're happy, we coo quietly. When we're not pleased, we're much louder. We either whine, meaning, 'I want' or 'come closer,' or we bellow, meaning 'go away' or 'take it away.' Much of our communication all through our lives is really about the same thing."

"Do you really think I can stop being so shy?" Lisa asked.

"Definitely," I responded.

"I notice that sometimes when I talk for a while," said June, "my voice begins to get hoarse."

"That's because you're using words," I replied.

There was some snickering.

"What's she supposed to do, grunt?" Tom asked.

"That might not be a bad idea," I replied. "Have any of you seen the film *Quest for Fire*?"

Lisa, Tom, and Duke raised their hands.

"The film is a wonderful portrayal of life in the Stone Age and the changes that are caused by the discovery of fire.

"These people haven't fully developed a language yet, and almost no words are spoken through the entire picture. But you can follow everything that's happening and know exactly how each character is feeling, because they are constantly expressing their feelings through sound. They are so expressive with their sounds and body language that words are unnecessary.

"I believe that we are designed to make sound. Emotions come out naturally in sounds—cooing, growling, moaning. Often, because of embarrassment or 'shoulds,' we exert our will to stop a sound from coming out the way it would naturally.

"Using words can strain the vocal mechanism because we are producing a series of short, clipped sounds which don't convey any emotion. Words often get in the way of a true expression of feeling. Often we talk and talk and never say what we really mean."

"I've done that often enough," added Duke.

"Or even if we do say what we mean, we often don't say it in the way we mean it. I can say, 'I am angry with you,' in a tone that conveys no anger at all. What I am concerned with is that words are used to express feelings, not to hide them. If I tell someone I am angry with him, or I like him, I want the feeling to be in my tone. *The voice works best when it is powered by passion.*"

"Most of what I say at work doesn't involve passion," remarked Bill. "I normally use words to explain something."

"They've done studies of audiences leaving a theater and found that people lose about seventy percent of the words. What they focus on is the plot and the emotions of the characters. *People pay much more attention to your tone of voice and what it conveys than they do to the words you say.*

"I am concerned in this class with teaching you to use words so that they come from your guts. That will put power and richness in your voices."

Feeling the Voice

"The more vibrations we produce, the more fully the vocal folds and the entire body are vibrating, the better the sound we make. I developed the work we're going to be doing to free our voices by combining Reichian theory with the insights and techniques of Kristan Linklater. Linklater, in her book, *Freeing the Natural Voice*, suggests that the more we pay attention to the *feeling of vibration*, wherever we notice it in the body, the fuller our sound will become. In other words, *instead of paying attention to how our voices sound, we are going to focus on how they feel.*"

"Why can't we pay attention to the sound itself?" asked Bill.

"Your voice produces vibrations which travel through the air and reach the ears of other people. But you hear your own voice partially from inside your head. Your voice on a tape recorder sounds like what other people hear."

"Ugh," Storm responded.

"It sounds particularly bad because you're not used to it. Since you can never really know what you sound like at the moment you're speaking, it's useless to try to hear yourself. Actually, it's worse than useless because it makes you self-conscious. Nothing helps you lose your voice faster than trying to sound good."

"That happens to me," said Bill. "Every couple of months, I get a sore throat. I'd love to get rid of it."

"We have already begun work on changing our voices," I responded. "After the last class, your voice was far more relaxed than it had been."

"It was?"

"I noticed that," said June. "It seemed easier to talk after class. Like I wasn't working so hard."

"A full sound corresponds to the amount of air which rushes past the vocal folds, so it relates directly to breathing. The second requirement is the looseness of the muscles so that the bones have a chance to vibrate fully.

"We have begun work in both of those areas. You are already experiencing gains from doing less. Now, we are going to add to what we've done. After the body movement exercise, we will work directly on increasing the quantity and quality of our vibrations."

Making Sound

I had my students lie on the floor and took them through a movement awareness exercise. After the exercise, when they were in a state of great awareness and relaxation, I began the Voice Visualization you will find in the Exercises section. I helped them to visualize themselves as very open and spacious, allowing all the air possible to fill them and empty out again. Then I encouraged them to *allow* an easy sound to come out of them, a sound made without effort, and to pay attention to any vibrations that they could see, hear, or feel.

The only sound I heard was from Bill, but it was forced and strained, not the "allowed" sound which I was seeking. As I walked around the room, I heard a soft, surprisingly low sound coming from Lisa. I pushed down gently on her chest and the sound grew louder.

Tom was also making a faint sound, far higher than any sound he made in talking. It was so soft I could only hear it when I leaned over him. His jaw was closed and his lips were close together so the sound came out as a hum. I gently pushed down on his jaw. He immediately opened it wide and held it there. "No," I told him, "let me do it." He let his jaw close again. I pushed gently with my fingers until it opened slightly.

June and Storm were making no sound, though they were breathing deeply. Duke had again fallen asleep.

After the exercise, the students came slowly to their feet where they stood, looking blissful and relaxed.

"How do you feel?" I asked.

"Stoned," replied Tom.

"I couldn't see any vibrations," said Storm.

"Neither could I," said Bill.

"That's okay," I replied. "The vibrations are only a gimmick, a way to get your concentration away from your throat and down deep into your guts where the sound forms."

"It sure feels good," Tom sighed.

Helping Each Other

The following week, I announced that we were

going to add a new element to the work.

"I've found that it is a lot easier to communicate to the body through touch than with words," I told the class, "so today you will pair up and help each other make sound."

"You mean we're going to touch each other?" asked Bill.

"Yes, gently. And only as much as you both feel comfortable with. Once we stop being children, our society allows us little opportunity to touch or be touched, except by a lover. Consequently, *most of us spend our lives suffering from touch hunger.*

"They have found with babies in orphanages that if they are not touched sufficiently, some of them will actually die. Juvenile delinquents will actually bring punishment on themselves, just to make sure they are touched, even if it's in a hostile way. As adults, we don't lose our need to be touched, we just deny it. And part of us shrivels up.

"In addition to working the voice, this class will give us a chance to fulfill some of our need to touch and be touched."

Bill still looked a little troubled.

"Sounds great to me," said Tom.

"It's a good opportunity to learn that touching doesn't have to be sexual."

"It doesn't?" asked Tom, in mock disappointment.

"No," I responded. "Touching can be a very effective way of communicating and teaching, without forcing the entire process to go through the verbal, rational left brain."

We went through the same sequence of body movement exercise and visualization. Then, I had the students pair up. As one was lying down, seeing and feeling vibrations, the other student was sitting alongside, near the first one's head, with the assignment of helping him make sound. "I don't know what I'm supposed to be doing," said Storm in some panic. She was sitting helplessly by Lisa's side, while Lisa allowed an easy sound to come out.

"You don't have to do anything. Believe it or not, just lying there with your eyes closed and making sounds can be very scary. Just having another person present is comforting. The most important thing you can do is be comfortable. And remember to keep breathing yourself. Then, once you're comfortable, you can help by gently touching the other person any place you see or sense tension. Especially, you can make sure the jaw stays open and you can press gently on the chest during the exhale, guiding it down.

"But remember that *you don't have to do anything*. In fact, don't do anything until you find your hands moving almost by themselves. We're working with empathy here, which is an intuitive ability. . . . Easy, Bill. He doesn't need all that help. Give yourself a chance to tune in."

"What's empathy?" Bill asked. He was pushing vigorously on Tom's chest as Tom was lying with his eyes closed.

"Empathy is feeling the same as someone else. Babies and young children have it to an astonishing degree. In fact, that's how they learn. They pick up whatever is going on with the adults around them; they can't be fooled. Empathy is also the main tool of actors and psychologists. When I tell you to breathe, it's usually because I notice that I've suddenly stopped breathing. . . . Now close your eyes. Just feel the connection."

"I don't feel any connection," said Bill.

"You will. Just give yourself a chance. It's just like with the sound. *You can't allow a sound to come if you keep trying to make sound.*"

After a while, the students reversed roles. Bill began sounding immediately, but the sound was forced.

"You're straining," I told him. "Do it easily."

He opened his eyes. "I'm doing it as easily as I can."

"Well, do it even more easily."

"I can't do it any more easily."

"Try."

"Try to do it more easily?" Tom asked, rolling his eyes.

Bill closed his eyes again. He lay there in frustration. I walked away to help the others.

As soon as she felt my presence, June opened her eyes. She smiled up at me self-consciously. "I keep on yawning," she said. "I can't seem to stop myself."

"That's fine."

"It is?" she asked, surprised.

"As I've said before, the only rules in the class on yawning are that you can't cover your mouth and that you have to make as much noise as you can."

June smiled and closed her eyes to resume the exercise.

I returned to Bill. He had relaxed considerably. In fact, he seemed less worried and controlled than I had ever seen him.

"Very nice," I said gently. "Very nice. Now, just easily let the breath go in and out. See the pool of vibrations." Very gently, I pushed on his chest. A tiny, infinitesimal sound came out. He breathed again. During the exhale I again pushed down his chest gently. The sound got a tiny bit louder. Bill opened his eyes.

"That's what you mean, isn't it?" he asked. "That was right, wasn't it?"

I nodded.

"I stopped trying and I did it. I allowed a sound to come." He was radiant.

"Yes, you did it."

"It's really simple, isn't it? You just kind of think about letting a sound out and breathe into the thought and it comes."

"That's right."

Bill was silent a minute, then his face clouded. "It isn't really much of an accomplishment, is it?"

"You'd be surprised," I replied.

EXERCISES

Before I give you the Voice Visualization exercise, let me say a few more words about the basic Body Awareness exercise you learned in the last chapter. *The actual movements you do are less important than the way you do them.* It is the ease of movement along with the focusing of full attention which allows these exercises to have their effect.

In a workshop I attended given by Moshe Feldenkrais, many people were asking for exercises to solve specific body problems (back pain, bad hip, etc.). Feldenkrais's reply was "The movements are only a trick. You could lie on your back and curl and uncurl your little finger for two hours, and if you could keep yourself focused, you would get the same results."

You can move any part of your body— gently, slowly, with detailed attention to the whole. You can experiment with different combinations of movements as long as they are pleasurable and seem to complement each other. You can begin with any easy movement and see where your body takes you.

From the work we did in the preceding chapter, it is easy to think of other possible combinations of simple movements. In the prior exercise, we worked the left shoulder and the right heel. You still have a right shoulder and a left heel, and you can repeat the prior exercise using them. You can also alternate raising the right and left shoulders. You can alternate moving the right and left heels. This one simple exercise has many possible variations.

There are also many possible simple individual movements to explore. You could press your shoulder gently into the ground instead of lifting it. You could extend your toes instead of your heels. You could attach an imaginary string to your knees or your elbows. The possibilities are infinite.

To get full benefit from this book, see if you can make this type of exercise a regular part of your life. There are teachers of Feldenkrais technique in many cities. And, as I said, you can make up your own exercises. Even ten or fifteen minutes every couple of days will help you free your mind of left-brain worries and regain a sense of ease and tranquility.

You will become aware of your body and shift your attention from concerns about the past or future to experiencing yourself fully in the present.

You can use a Body Awareness exercise to lead into the Voice Visualization exercise, as I do in my class.

Voice Visualization

This visualization, derived from the one developed by Kristan Linklater, is designed to help you free your body of tension, to deepen your breathing, and to begin *allowing a sound to come*

out without any effort. I recommend using this
Visualization constantly and integrating it into
your life. Once you begin to sound, you can
continue to do so for as long as you like, provided it remains easy and pleasurable. Any
pushing or trying to make the sound will defeat
the purpose of the exercise. You may not make
any sound the first several times you do this,
as the whole concept of making sound without
effort is a very difficult one for us. At some
point, however, sound will come, and you will
be amazed at how easy it is.

As far as voice production is concerned,
you have no throat. While this is not literally accurate, it is essential to locate the sound forma-
tion deep down in your center, where the
impulse to breathe begins. You can think of
either a hollow tube running from your lower
abdomen to your face or you can allow the
vibrations to run along your spine, up over the
top of your head and out your nose and mouth.

During the sounding which comes out of
this exercise, it is important to *allow the jaw to
drop open.* This does not mean holding it open,
which is not very different from holding it
closed. Rather, just allow it to drop. For now,
you might press gently on your jaw with a finger until it moves slightly back and down to
accustom it to dropping. If your jaw refuses
to open, don't worry about it. It will open at
a later stage.

In my class, I have my students pair up

and help each other do this exercise. While this is definitely not necessary, it can be very helpful. If you have a spouse, lover, or friend whom you can interest in sharing this exercise with you, you will be doing both them and yourself a great service. Then one of you can help while the other "allows" sound. For suggestions on how to help each other most effectively, you can reread the section Helping Each Other.

Visualization

Lie comfortably on your back on a foam pad or a well-carpeted floor with your arms at your sides and your eyes closed. Feel how your body is resting against the floor, which parts are touching, which parts aren't touching. Monitor your breathing. Begin to scan your skeleton easily, visualizing the bones in your feet, your ankles. . . .

See your shin bones; see your kneecaps just floating there. Just let them float.

And see your thigh bones, and the way they fit into your hip joints.

See your pelvis, and let it spread out and widen across the floor.

And see your tailbone. See it come through your pelvis and emerge in those large vertebrae of the lower lumbar region of the spine. Good large vertebrae that can support you.

Begin to walk up your spine, vertebra by

vertebra, seeing lots of space between each
vertebra.

And then you come to the vertebrae where
the ribs attach.

See a pair of ribs attaching at each vertebra. Let them be very soft, like foam rubber.

First you have the two pair of floating ribs.

And then the ten pair of ribs that connect
at the breastbone.

Let the breastbone also be as soft as foam
rubber.

See your shoulder blades and your shoulder girdle, and let those spread out and widen
across the floor.

See the bones in your arms—your upper
arms, your forearms, wrists, hands, fingers—
with lots of space in each joint.

Then go back to the place between your
shoulder blades where the neck joins the
shoulders.

Walk up the vertebrae of your neck, vertebra by vertebra. See lots of space between
each vertebra.

You have seven vertebrae in your neck, as
many as a giraffe has. So see your neck as long
and flowing as a giraffe's.

And then see your skull just floating on the
top.

See the muscles of your face from the inside.

Let them dissolve and melt away.

The muscles in your jaw and in your cheeks.

The muscles around your eyes and in your scalp.

And begin to see spaces.

See a space in your forehead, a space at the base of your skull.

See a space going down your neck.

Space in your shoulders and down your arms.

See space going down your back.

Space in your ribs.

Space in the small of your back.

Space in your lower abdomen.

Space in your groin.

Space in your buttocks.

Space in your inner thighs and all the way down your legs.

And let the air come in and fill all these spaces.

You don't have to do anything; it just fills you up.

And your whole body is open and spacious.

As the air fills you, your body expands.

As the air goes out, your body contracts, and you get that basic rhythm of expansion and contraction.

The rhythm of all life.

Just feel the air coming in and filling you and going out.

You don't have to do anything.

And now I'd like you to see, or hear, or feel a pool of vibrations deep down inside you.

These vibrations have a color and a texture.
They buzz and hum.
They can be any image that works for you.
They can be a swarm of yellow bees buzzing.
Or black crows flying.
Or squiggles of blue electricity.
Or a can of pink, wiggly worms.
Or a fiery orange sun.
Or silver champagne bubbles.
Any image that works for you.
Locate these vibrations deep down in your
lower abdomen, in your groin, in your thighs.
The breath drops in and touches the vibra-
tions, which begin to buzz and hum.
They buzz and hum up your spine and out
your nose and mouth.
And the sound, when it's ready to come
out, is an easy sigh of relief.
Take your time.
Take all the trying out of it.
Just keep seeing the vibrations.
Letting a breath drop in and disturb them.
They start to buzz and hum.
They buzz and hum up your spine.
And the sound is an easy sigh of relief.
Keep seeing the vibrations and letting the
breath drop in and disturb them.
And remember that whatever happens is
okay.
If no sound comes, that's fine.
If you start to yawn, let yourself.
If you start to laugh because the whole thing

seems silly, that's fine.

Just keep seeing the vibrations.

And keep letting the breath drop down.

And the sound, when it's ready, is an easy sigh of relief.

You can do this exercise as long as it is pleasurable and comfortable. When you have had enough, let your sound fade out and just rest. You can yawn and stretch if you want to. Allow your eyes to open slowly. Then slowly roll to the side and come to a sitting position, using your head as little as possible.

You may find yourself a little woozy after this exercise, so allow yourself some time to recover. After you do this for a while, you will find your voice to be deeper and more relaxed than you had ever thought possible.

Taking It Further

Once you have gotten the hang of this exercise, you will want to use it all the time. As you get the knack, you will need less and less induction time and be able to go right into allowing sound without needing the visualization.

As you continue this work, you may find that your sounds get louder. They may actually escalate into screams and groans. At times you may worry what the neighbors think. Just let them know that you are practicing an unusual voice technique. That will satisfy their curiosity and probably keep them from calling the police.

A great place to do this work is while driving (with your eyes open, of course, and with proper attention to the road). The car has become the only really private place left for most people in America. "Sounding" has gotten me through many a boring drive and many a traffic jam on Los Angeles freeways.

RESULTS

The following week, we began class by discussing the changes the students had noticed. June was excited:

"The next day after the class, my husband called me from his office and he didn't recognize my voice, it was so low. He thought he had the wrong number."

"That's great," I said.

"But by the day after it was back to normal."

"Yeah," said Bill. "My voice stayed relaxed for the next two days, but after that it began to tense up again. And I could feel it tensing up, but there just wasn't anything I could do about it."

"It's very frustrating," said June, "to feel it change back and not be able to keep it."

"It's the same thing that happened with Duke's posture," I replied. "We're trying to change years of habit. Using these techniques, it's really not that hard to get your voice and body to change. *The trick is keeping them changed.*

That's why I have us work slowly and gradually.

"It's wonderful to have changes as dramatic as Duke's or June's, but often the changes are subtle and small at first. And people may not even notice them. For instance. . ." I turned to Lisa. "Has anyone told you that your face looks different?"

"No," Lisa replied.

"Well, it does. Does anyone notice anything?"

Everybody looked at Lisa, making her extremely uncomfortable.

"Yes, there is something different," Duke said. "I can't quite put it into words."

"She looks softer," said June. "More open."

"Yeah, that's it," Duke agreed.

"Her cheeks have let go a little, right in here," said Tom, indicating his own face just below his eyes. "And her eyes are shining more."

Lisa closed her eyes and looked away.

"Are you okay?" I asked her.

"Yes," she said. "It just embarrasses me to have everyone looking at me."

"Why?" asked Tom.

"I don't know. It just does."

"Another important function of this class will be giving each other feedback, so that we learn how our progress shows to other people. The changes that we're noticing now," I continued, "are subtle ones. You'll find the comments you will get from other people will be, 'Have you changed your hairstyle?' or 'Have you lost weight?'"

"I don't feel very positive," said Storm. "I'm sick of being so tight. I keep trying to fix my body and it just doesn't get any better."

"Where do you feel tight?" I asked.

"Everywhere. Especially my neck and shoulders."

"Is there anywhere you feel loose?"

"No."

"Anywhere? Even a little loose?"

"Well, my stomach doesn't feel as tight as the rest of me," Storm admitted.

"Good. I want you to go in there. Close your eyes and just keep paying attention to your stomach. See the looseness. Can you see a color?"

"Red," Storm replied.

"Good. Keep seeing the red and letting it grow and spread. Let it fill your body. Can you do that?"

"Yes."

"Okay, now slowly bring your attention back to your neck and shoulders. Do they feel any different?"

"They feel a little looser," Storm admitted tentatively.

"It's amazing how we always pay attention to where we're tight," I commented. "What does that attention do?"

"Makes you tighter," Tom commented.

"Exactly. I'd like to make a suggestion that, as much as you can, *you always focus on what's right about you rather than what's wrong with you.*

Concentrate on where you feel good rather than where you feel bad."

"I have something to report also," said Tom. "I've started moaning and sighing all the time. People are looking at me like I'm weird."

"What's new about that?" Duke put in, smirking.

"When I was teaching college," I responded, "the students used to look at me very peculiarly when I began to sigh. After a while, they got used to it. I remember that one of my colleagues at school told me that he would get so tight at lectures that he would get a headache, and he asked me what he should do.

" 'Yawn,' I told him.

" 'Oh, no,' he said, 'that would be rude. Isn't there anything else?' "

"I told him he could also sigh or groan, but these didn't strike him as any better, so he was left with his headache. We sigh and yawn naturally, especially when we're bored, so that we can take in new air and energize our systems. But yawning and sighing do make people in our society uncomfortable."

"It's not easy to do this work and be polite," Tom said.

"I would just say that there's a balance to maintain," I responded. "Generally, we pay far too much attention to what other people may think. In performance terms, we call that 'stage-fright.' Our restrained, tightened voices are clear evidence of the tyranny of other people's opinions. This work is aimed at helping you all get over your stagefright and connect more with the freedom and satisfaction that comes with full self-expression."

5

EMOTIONS: DOWN-FALL OR SALVATION?

Our voices, breathing patterns, and all the muscles of our bodies are designed to express our feelings. When we try to control our emotions by resisting their expression or denying their existence, we are fighting against our very nature. Unexpressed emotions get stuck in our bodies and never go away. They are stored as muscular tension and chemical imbalance, which can literally make us sick. The full expression of an emotion releases it and allows us to move on. We feel more alive, more peaceful. And we can communicate better with others because we are not hiding or stifling ourselves.

Learning to express our feelings in a safe and useful way is the fourth step to personal power. We are built to experience the full range of emotions. When you allow them to, emotions flow through you in a natural rhythm. You can learn to gently guide them, determining when, where, and how they will be

expressed. When you express and let go of
feelings as they arise, your body feels lighter,
your breathing becomes freer, your voice fuller.
Emotions become a more comfortable and
integrated. part of your life.

Laughing and Crying

After the fourth class, Storm had announced,
smiling, that she didn't know why, but she would
like to punch me in the nose. At the fifth class,
she reported she had been irritable all week,
snapping at her employees and avoiding her
friends. Storm still held her chest raised way
up in the air, like a little girl trying to look
bigger. She hardly seemed to breathe. At this
point, she was the only one who had not made
any sound.

As she lay on the floor after the usual visualization, not sounding and hardly breathing,
I came over and began to press down on her
chest slowly but forcefully. Gradually, her chest
began to release and move. Her eyes filled with
tears and she began to cry quietly. As soon as
she felt the tears, however, Storm tensed her
face in a valiant effort to contain them.

"Let your face go," I said gently.

"No," she responded.

"You'll feel better."

"I don't want you to see me like this. I don't
want anybody to see me like this."

"We won't look."

"I don't want to cry."

"Why not?"

"I'm afraid."

"What are you afraid of?"

"I'm afraid I'll never stop."

"You'll stop. You'll cry for a while, then you'll stop. Otherwise you'll keep those tears forever."

I began to massage her forehead gently. Gradually, the tears came. I pressed on her chest again and she began to sob—high-pitched sobs, like those of a little baby.

Bill opened his eyes and sat up. I went over to him.

"Is she all right?" he asked.

"She's all right."

"Shouldn't someone be taking care of her?"

"She's taking care of herself."

June also opened her eyes and I told her to go on working. Then Lisa began to sob—deep, rich sobs, much louder than Storm's. Lisa was able to cry easily; tears ran down her cheeks.

As the two women continued crying, Tom began to laugh; it was a deep, infectious laugh, which filled the room. His laugh would die down for a minute, then start up again. Soon, Duke began to laugh, also. Bill sat up again.

"What's going on here anyway?"

"I don't know . . . I can't help. . ." Tom managed before he was overwhelmed by laughter again.

As the laughter continued, the crying got

more intense.

"How the hell can I make sound with all this noise going on?" Bill asked indignantly.

Tom let out an even louder laugh. Duke followed suit. The crying redoubled.

"Well, I'm trying to improve myself. If the women have to cry, let them. But Tom certainly doesn't have to laugh like that."

"Mature adults," Duke put in, "lying on the floor, moaning." He began to laugh again. Lisa began to laugh also. She went back to crying, then laughed again. Soon, it was impossible to tell which she was doing.

"Are you laughing or crying?" I asked her.

"I don't know," she replied, "but it sure feels good."

Eventually, the tumult died down and we formed a circle to discuss what had happened.

"Did you know why you were crying?" June asked Storm.

Storm shook her head. "I just felt very sad . . . What did you do to me?" she asked me with some anger in her voice. "I didn't want to cry."

"I wasn't trying to get you to cry. I was just pressing down on your chest to help you allow sound to come. The crying was your idea."

"It was not."

"You see, you hold your chest way up in the air and hold your breath in order to keep all the tears in. You can't just allow sound to come out because you have so much unexpressed emotion locked in your chest that it gets in the way. When I finally got your chest to move, you fought the tears by tightening your forehead until you gave yourself a headache. When I got you to relax your forehead, the tears came."

"That's true," Storm admitted.

"How do you feel now?"

"Better," Storm conceded. "Peaceful. But I'm still angry with you."

"Okay, you can be angry."

"Thank you," Storm said sarcastically.

"I feel a lot lighter," said Lisa. "Like a weight's been taken off."

"I feel really awesome," Tom put in. "My whole body is tingling again. What a rush."

"Wait a minute," said Bill. "Are you really saying that Storm literally has tears stored in her chest and these tears keep her from making sound?"

"Literally, Storm's tears are held in her tear ducts above her eyes. Releasing her chest began a whole process which led to her crying.

"We began to talk last week about Wilhelm Reich's theory of 'character armor' which involves tensing muscles in order to keep from expressing or even feeling emotions. The way Storm holds her chest is part of her character armor, as is the tightness in her forehead.

"Though each individual is unique, there are places where we are more likely to block certain emotions. We talked two weeks ago of how the jaw and the buttocks often hold rage. Tightened shoulders can also indicate anger, a restraint of the impulse to strike. The diaphragm and the stomach often hold sadness. If you notice where you tighten when you feel a particular emotion, you'll get a sense of what is blocked when that area is held tight."

I could see my students considering this, turning their attention inward and checking out their own bodies.

"I should also mention that there are two parts to crying: shedding tears, which actually cleanses the system, and making sound, which attracts attention. Lisa and Storm seem much better at shedding tears than at making sound; this is not uncommon in women. For myself, I've been able to cry noisily for a few years now, but it's only recently that I began shedding tears."

"You mean that you cry?" asked Bill, his upper lip curling slightly.

"Whenever I can," I responded. "It's still hard for me."

"I wish I could cry," Tom said wistfully.

"Why do you want to?" Bill asked both of us.

Expressing Emotions

"We are meant to express our emotions. Our voices, tear ducts, and all the muscles in our bodies are meant to be powered by—and expressive of—feelings. As sound begins to come up, emotions come up with it, as they did for Storm. That's why we usually don't allow ourselves simply to make sound. We are afraid of what we will reveal. We have been taught to carefully edit ourselves."

Lisa looked at me with interest. Tom nodded approval. The others looked puzzled.

"What about all the laughter?" Bill asked.

"That was also an expression of emotion," I replied.

"I felt that he was laughing at me," said Storm. "It made me angry."

"I don't think he was laughing at you," I replied, "though I do feel that your crying triggered Tom's laughter just as it triggered Lisa's tears."

"It upset me when the women started to cry," Tom admitted. "I'm really not comfortable with tears. I felt really charged up and it came out as laughter."

"We think of laughter and crying as opposites in terms of the emotion each releases. However, if you look at someone's body when they laugh or cry, you'll see that the rib cage goes down, the neck arches back and the pelvis thrusts forward. What happens in the face is different, but the body movement is basically the same."

"By the end, I didn't know whether I was laughing or crying," said Lisa.

"Neither did I. You see, people are often

afraid that if they start to express an emotion, like sadness, they have so much stored up, it will take forever to let it all out. However, emotions are naturally transitory; they move through you and out. And once the emotion is discharged, another comes to take its place.

"I have had students laugh until they started crying, and I have had students cry until all their sadness suddenly seemed ridiculous to them and they started laughing. It's like a magician's magic hat, from which one brightly colored handkerchief after the other appears. Whenever I feel caught in one emotion, I try to see it as a wave washing through me."

"I hate feeling out of control like that," Bill said.

"The problem for many people when they experience emotions is that they feel 'out of control.' What is actually not in control is the logical, rational left brain. The rest of the brain is right in there, doing its job."

"You see," I continued, "*emotions, like posture, breathing, movement, and sounding, are automatic functions of the body.* In fact, the limbic system, which largely regulates emotions, is located in the right brain just in front of the hind brain, which regulates automatic physical functions. By electrically stimulating the emotional center of the brain, the entire range of emotions can be produced.

"*Emotions are brain-induced chemical changes in the body. The chemical changes which correspond to fear, anger, sadness, or joy lead to certain physical responses:* if we are scared, we may start to tremble and break out in a cold sweat; if we are sad, our chests heave and tears well up in our eyes; when we are angry, our body temperature rises, our fists clench and strike out, and our jaw muscles may tighten—otherwise we may bite or scream."

Emotion Phobia

"Unfortunately," I went on, "we live in an emotion-phobic society. As children, we quickly learn that certain emotions, or maybe even all emotions, are not 'okay.' So we begin to hold them back. Sometimes, it even starts as a conscious decision. I remember deciding when I was about five years old that I wouldn't give anyone the satisfaction of seeing me cry, and I never cried again until I began doing this work."

"When I used to cry," June said, "my father would yell at me to stop crying or he'd give me something to cry about."

"That happened to me, too," Duke said.

Lisa looked like she wanted to say something, so I asked her if she did. She hesitated for a minute, then spoke haltingly:

"My father left home when I was three. I used to cry about it all the time. I used to pray to God that he would come back. Then I decided I wouldn't cry for him any more. It just hurt too much."

There was a silence.

"Thank you for telling us that," I said. "Would anyone else like to share? Any other emotions besides sadness?"

"My parents used to yell at each other all the time," Duke said. "I decided that I didn't want to be like that."

"My parents always told me not to be silly," said Bill. "They didn't like it when I kidded around."

"I remember in school, in fourth grade, I just couldn't stop giggling," said June. "I don't know why. I couldn't help it. The teacher made me stay after school—'until you learn to control yourself and behave properly,' she said." June's eyes misted over at the memory.

"Why are adults so stupid?" Lisa asked.

"Most adults are terribly uncomfortable with their own emotions," I responded. "As a result, they are just as uncomfortable with their children's feelings—or those of other adults, for that matter."

"Why is that?" Duke asked.

"*Emotions are contagious.* You experienced that during the voice work. Once Storm started crying, all hell broke loose. When adults see children emoting, it brings up their own emotions, which they have denied for so long and which they are no longer equipped to handle without losing self-image. Emotion-phobia is self-perpetuating. You will find that as it becomes easier for you to accept your own emotions through this work, it will be easier for you to accept other people's."

"But emotions can be dangerous," Bill contended. "Like you said before about anger making you want to hit and bite. What if I got angry at you and grabbed you and started punching?"

"Emotions are not dangerous; certain ways of expressing them are. My own belief is that people who get physically violent do not have the ability to express their emotions in a more direct and harmless manner. Part of being an adult is that we have some choice in how, when, and where we are going to express our emotions."

"But you said that emotions involve chemical changes that lead inevitably to certain expressions," Bill continued. "Like trembling if we're nervous."

"We do have choice in guiding our emotional expression. What is important is that we acknowledge it to ourselves and find some way to let it come out."

"Why is that so important?" asked June.

The Danger of Non-Expression

"Let me go back to the child who begins to hide his feelings. He may do this because the adult world will not stand for them. Or he may have the dilemma Bill suggested and not be able to conceive of expressing his anger except in a violent and destructive way.

"In either case, he begins to tense his muscles against the impulse to laugh, cry, or get angry. Gradually, the channels of expression begin to close. The whole body goes into a holding pattern, designed to keep everything inside. In addition to tensing muscles, we also begin to restrict our breathing. As I showed you earlier, the two go together.

"When breathing is restricted, we actually feel less. As a result, we are afraid to release emotions not only for the physical consequences, but because our bodies are no longer equipped for the physical changes which are produced. That feeling we get of not being able to 'bear' an emotion has some physical truth.

"Meanwhile, *even when we are no longer expressing our emotions, even when we have deadened ourselves enough so that we no longer feel them, the chemical, physical changes are still taking place in our bodies.* If we don't express our emotions, these chemical changes produce poisons. Toxins build up in the muscles and organs. If the toxins are not expelled from the body, the result is not unlike heating gas in an airtight container: sooner or later, there will be an explosion."

"What kind of explosion?" asked Bill.

"Back aches, headaches, nervous tics, all the way up to nervous breakdowns, and, some studies indicate, even strokes and cancer."

"Just from not expressing our emotions?" Bill asked.

"Is there really evidence?" asked June. "I mean, I know they've related a lot of ailments like headaches and arthritis to stress."

" 'Stress' is really the nonemotional word for anxiety. And there is nothing more stressful and anxiety-producing than not expressing your emotions. Since stress is related directly to outside stimuli, its effect can be verified more easily. Let me put it this way: lack of emotional expression can be an important factor in developing illness."

Suddenly Tom screamed at Duke: "Did I ever tell you you were a lousy piece of scum!"

Everyone stared at Tom.

"I figured I'd better get those toxins out before it was too late," he said, smiling sweetly.

Masculine and Feminine: Emotional Range

"I can't believe you just did that," Storm said to Tom.

"Hey, I was just kidding around."

"Well, it wasn't very funny."

"I was just kidding around," Tom repeated. "Duke knows I was just kidding around, don't you?"

Duke considered it a moment, then launched himself at Tom and the two began to wrestle. At first, the rest of us were worried, but it quickly became clear that they were enjoying each other. The play-fight ended when

Duke had Tom's arms pinned on the ground and Tom cried "uncle." They both got up looking extremely satisfied with themselves. It was clear a new friendship had been cemented.

June turned to me. "Does this sort of thing happen often in your classes?"

"Not very often," I admitted. "At least not this early in the sequence. But many people are disconcerted by the amount of laughter and general rowdiness that goes on in my classes. I figure that the majority have more than enough restrictions most of the time. I tend to lean over backward to create an environment where people can do what they want."

"Tom doesn't seem to have any trouble expressing emotions and impulses," said June.

"What was so funny?" Bill asked Tom.

"I don't know," Tom replied. "It didn't really strike me as funny until after I started laughing. I mean the laughing struck me as funny, but the laughing at first was something else. Does that make sense?"

"Not much." Bill replied.

"What I heard in Tom's laugh was power," I said. "I call that kind of laugh, which I hear a lot in class and rarely anywhere else, a *power laugh. It relates to someone looking deep inside himself and really getting a sense of his own power.*"

"I did feel very powerful," Tom said. "I felt that I could do what I wanted to and no one could stop me."

"That deep primitive laughter is often the

first emotional expression which comes up for people doing this work. Interestingly enough, the laughter comes up much more often for men. For women, crying is usually the first expression of emotion, as we saw with Storm."

"Why is that?" June asked.

"I think it relates to our social roles. As I said before, *men are more comfortable with feeling powerful, women are more comfortable with vulnerable feelings.*

"*We all feel and have a need to express the entire range of emotions.* Certain people are more comfortable expressing certain emotions. The most common societal channeling of emotions is that girls can cry and boys can rage. However, acceptable emotions vary tremendously from family to family and even within each family. While crying and anger are the emotional outlets most commonly prohibited, there are people who feel that life is a serious business and that it is inappropriate to laugh."

Everyone looked at Bill.

"Hey, don't look at me," he responded. "I can laugh as much as the next guy. I was just trying to get some work done."

"Present company always excepted," I responded.

"And accepted," added June. "We'll accept you, Bill, even if you do think life is a serious business."

"I don't think . . . ," Bill began. Then he stopped himself. "Yeah, I guess I do."

"Many people have been brought up so that only one emotion is acceptable," I continued. One of my female students a number of years ago was only comfortable with feeling and expressing anger; when she was hurt, she felt angry; when she was sad, she felt angry. Because I was at the time completely unable to express my own anger, and all she could express was anger, we were fascinated by each other."

The Joy of Emoting

"I can pretend to be angry," said Tom, "like I did with Duke before. But it's hard for me to really get angry—to really feel it. I guess laughing and joking around are the only emotions that come easily for me."

"You sure know how to laugh," June put in.

"Well, I don't usually laugh like that," Tom replied. "After I laughed, I felt so full of energy and so rowdy I just had to do something. That's why I got goofy with Duke."

"What was the laughing about for you, Duke?" I asked.

"Well, I started laughing because Tom was laughing. I felt like I had caught it from him."

"Earlier, I said that emotions are contagious. It's the result of empathy, which I talked about last week. When someone is feeling something strongly, we begin to feel it also. That's what an actor uses to 'get inside' his character and what the audience uses to identify with the actor. We flock to the theatre and films largely because actors portray such strong feelings that they seem more alive than we are, and watching them makes us empathize and consequently feel more alive.

"Laughter is the most contagious of emotions. It feels so good that our bodies imitate it as soon as they sense it. It's like yawning. You know how when someone in a room yawns, everyone starts to yawn? That's because we see someone yawning and our bodies become jealous. They want to stretch and release also.

"While laughter is the most obviously pleasurable, *the full expression of any emotion, no matter how painful the emotion, leaves us with some feeling of serenity and release. The severe pain we sometimes feel when we are in an emotional state is caused by our body fighting the emotion.* If we can let the emotion flow through us and out, as if it were a wave, we will always feel better."

"Wait a minute," Bill responded. "Are you saying it feels good to cry and get angry?"

"Isn't that like saying it feels good to feel miserable?" Tom asked.

"Not exactly. Sadness or anger or anxiety can be very unpleasant feelings. If someone you love dies, the feeling is certainly not pleasant. What I am saying is that expressing the feeling of grief will ease it and actually give you some comfort. The discharge of the feeling is pleasurable.

"For years, whenever I would get even a little bit angry, my whole body would begin to shake. The shaking was a battle between my anger and my attempt to hold it back. Now, when I get angry, I really enjoy it."

"Stay away from me, man!" said Tom with mock concern.

"I can guide my anger. I know I won't go 'out of my head' and cause violence. That's why I can enjoy it."

"I wish I could feel that way about it," said Duke. "I'm always scared I'll lose control and take someone's head off."

"I'm sure you could do it. I would be afraid to rile you, especially because of the way you clench your teeth and barely use your voice."

"Why is that?" Duke asked.

"One of the main places people hold anger is in the jaw. Anybody grind your teeth when you sleep?"

Duke indicated he did, as did June.

"That's generally a sign of held-back rage."

"What's the connection with the voice?" Duke asked.

"*Just as the body is designed to strike, the voice is designed to scream out anger. The more you learn to let the anger out with your voice, the less physical the discharge has to be.* One of Freud's great lines was that the man who hurled a curse instead of a rock at his opponent was the founder of civilization."

Guiding Your Anger: The Value of Fantasy

After class had ended, as students were getting their belongings together to leave, Storm came up to me with a menacing smile.

"You know, I'm still mad at you," she said. "I'd really like to punch you."

"Well, I don't think I'd like it much. Is there anything else you could do?"

"How about breaking all the windows?"

"No."

"I thought there weren't any rules here."

"You just found one of them. . . . All right, it would be okay with me if you hit me . . ."

Storm lit up and drew back her arm.

"With one condition." I picked up a large pillow and threw it down near her. "This is me."

Storm looked chagrined. "That's only a lousy pillow."

"But your unconscious doesn't know that. That's the wonderful thing about the emotions. They demand expression, but they're not much concerned about where or when."

By now the others saw that something was up and they clustered around.

"I can't just hit a lousy pillow. It's just not the same thing."

"Try it."

Storm bent over, lifted one arm, and made a halfhearted attempt to hit the pillow.

"You can do better than that," Tom shouted.

Storm swung at him, but he stepped back. She started for him.

"Wait a minute," I said. "He's the pillow too."

Storm turned to the pillow again, kneeled down, and hit it, hard. She stopped. "Hey, that felt pretty good," she said.

"Don't stop now."

"I feel silly."

"Do it anyway."

"What'sa matter, you chicken?" Tom shouted from a safe distance.

Storm went after the pillow with a vengeance. She rained blows on it, right- and left-handed. "You bastard," she shrieked in a high, almost inaudible voice, "you bastard!"

When she got tired, she threw herself on the pillow and rested.

"How do you feel now?" I asked.

"Much better," she said. "But I still feel a little silly."

"That looked great," said Tom. "When do we get to do it?"

"Whenever you want." Looking around, I could see that June looked troubled.

"Is something wrong?" I asked.

"It scared me," she replied. "I don't like violence. I saw too much of it when I was growing up."

"Okay, I can understand why it would scare you. But remember that all Storm hit was a pillow."

"I thought you said it was you," Tom put in.

"It's only me for as long as it needs to be. Then it becomes a pillow again. . . . I've been talking all class about guiding the discharge of emotion; this is a perfect example."

"But does it really get rid of the emotion?" asked Duke.

"Storm, do you still want to hit me?"

"Yes . . . no. A lot less than I did before. I feel pretty peaceful actually," Storm said, still lying on the pillow.

"Since the unconscious doesn't know time or place, fantasy can be a tremendous tool for guiding emotional discharge. Children discharge their emotion in fantasy all the time. It's one of the important purposes of playing. An example is a child striking a doll and saying, 'Bad Mommy, bad Mommy!' As adults, most of us have lost touch with the cathartic and health-promoting effects of play and fantasy. We've forgotten that *we can do absolutely anything in fantasy; it is only our actual behavior that we are responsible to others for.*

"I'd like to give you one example of how effective using fantasy can be. I had a student who had adopted a little girl. She was single and the strain of taking care of the child had really gotten to her. She was furious; she felt drained and pulled on all the time. She was actually thinking of returning the girl to the adoption center, a thought which made her feel even more guilty and inadequate. Her worry was such that she couldn't sleep at night. This had forced her to take a leave from her job.

"I suggested that she wait till the girl was in school, then really indulge in the fantasy of getting rid of her, of telling her what a lousy, inconsiderate child she was and how her mother wouldn't put up with it anymore. After she practiced this for a few weeks, she found her rage toward the child dwindling, and her love coming to the surface again. Since she didn't feel so guilty, she was able to discipline her child more effectively. Therefore, she had less resentment at the child for making unreasonable demands.

"She was able to cope with and enjoy the child on a day-to-day basis without getting caught in the trap of either being the perfect mother or returning the girl to the adoption center. Her insomnia gradually disappeared, and she was able to return to work."

"But what about really crazy people?" asked June. "Don't they often have violent fantasies and then act on them?"

"That's true. And the difference between us and them is that we can be content with just having the fantasies without acting on them."

"But how do we know we won't?"

"For psychotics, many times the fantasies come unbidden and actually take them over. Psychotics either live in their fantasies or unsuccessfully try to fight them off. The sys tem I'm advocating suggests giving the fantasies full rein—in their own domain—but recognizing and developing the distinction between fantasy and the real world. I'm talking about creating a safe space, then allowing the fantasies to come and the body to discharge anger.

"Storm knows that I am not that pillow. But for the moment, she could behave as if I was. I was not at all hurt, while she gained the satisfaction of discharging her anger. As you continue in the class and your bodies get looser, it will be easier and easier to discharge emotion."

"You mean we learn to hit the pillow better?" asked Tom.

"You could put it that way. My work frees your body so that as emotions begin to emerge they can rise naturally to the surface. It is extremely difficult for many people to release anger spontaneously at a person, let alone at an object. Many therapists advocate hitting a pillow instead of smacking your mother-in-law or murdering your boss. While I obviously believe in this approach, I think it's important that *your body is loose enough to discharge the anger effectively.*"

Emotional Breakthroughs

The following week, Duke threw a tantrum. He was lying on the floor, breathing and sounding, and he began to exhale and sound with increasing ferocity. I went over to him and, the next time his chest went down as he exhaled, I held it there. That was all it took. Suddenly, Duke started to move in all directions at once. His arms and legs were flailing. I quickly put pillows under his hands and feet and the pounding increased. Even Duke's pelvis was raised and then pounded against the floor.

"Good. Go for it. Use your voice!" I yelled.

Along with the pounding, Duke began to scream. His voice was still breathy, but there was more sound than I had ever heard from him before. After a few minutes he stopped and lay still. His face broke out into a big grin.

"How do you feel?" I asked.

"Wonderful," he answered in a new voice.

During the seventh class, Bill caught the fever and began pounding with his arms against the pillows. He screamed in a high, strained voice. Both his arms and voice behaved as if he were trying to get rid of something. His whole body did not get involved, so he didn't get the sense of completion that Duke had felt, but he seemed pleased with himself.

Lisa kept on the borderline of laughing and crying, each in turn getting louder and more fully expressed. Her jaw began to quiver. I massaged her jaw muscles and the quiver turned into full-fledged shaking. She lay there for a while with her jaw shaking, then she came up to a sitting position, grabbed a pillow that was near her and very methodically began to pound the living daylights out of it. When she was too tired to move her arms anymore, she lay down and rested. Her jaw was still quivering.

After her initial resistance, Storm had begun crying in earnest. She was afraid it would never stop.

Tom was still basically laughing and making funny noises. He was impressed by the women crying and expressed a wish to cry, but tears eluded him.

Of them all, only June was not expressing any emotion. This was beginning to distress her.

The Last Holdout: Freeing the Face

During our closing circle, June began to complain that she wasn't feeling any emotions.

"Everyone else seems to be having all these wonderful, dramatic things happen to them, but I don't seem to do anything. I just lie there and make sound."

"First of all, *there is no reason you have to emote*. This work is about *allowing what happens to happen*. There is no 'right' way to do it. The danger with watching other people is that you think you have to do it their way. It becomes yet another way to put ourselves down—and, God knows, we have enough put-downs."

"But I don't feel I'm getting anywhere."

"Different people learn and progress in many

ways. The most important thing I can teach you is to learn to accept your own rhythm."

"Actually, I'm a lot more comfortable not expressing a lot of emotion. I just feel like maybe I'm missing something."

"You need what's comfortable for you. In a few weeks, we'll get into a whole different way of looking at what we are trying to do, a way which sees emotions only as a byproduct. For now, though, there is something I can tell you which may begin to give you more access to your emotions."

"Am I going to like it?" June asked.

"I don't know. What I need to talk to you about is your smile. You have a fixed smile which you wear pretty much all the time. It is hard for you to express the different feelings you are going through when your face is always smiling."

"I've been told that I smile a lot," June agreed.

"I used to smile all the time," I told her.

"People always told me what a nice smile I had. When I got angry, I would only smile more, like this. . ." I said, baring all my teeth in a slightly maniacal grin. Everyone laughed.

"Seriously, that's what I used to do. Then I went to a Reichian marathon session and people there told me that I looked like a shark— all teeth. I was asked to go around the room and say something straight to each person without smiling to soften it. By the time I got through, my upper lip was quivering.

"Later that evening, I was talking to the group and a woman who always hogged the group's attention interrupted. She began talking about herself, as usual. As I sat there, one of my friends in the group pointed out that I was smiling again. Then, I deliberately let the smile go.

"The next thing I knew, I was telling the woman how angry I was to be interrupted and how rude and insensitive she was being. So help me, before I dropped the smile, I hadn't even known I was angry.

"Since then, I've made a conscious effort to get rid of my permanent smile."

Several of my students wiped smiles off their faces.

"Does that mean we're not supposed to smile?" asked Storm.

"Along with the voice, the face is our primary means of expressing ourselves and communicating with others. There are a great many muscles in the face, proportionately many more than there are anywhere else in the body. These are designed for expression. Our faces are designed to reflect our inner feelings; they are capable of a wide range of expression.

"As the rest of the body becomes free of tension, it is often the face which continues to hold on. After all, the rest of our bodies are usually hidden by clothes; they are less likely to reveal what is going on inside us to the world.

When the face changes, however, everybody sees. In its public nature, it is like the voice.

"Many people keep their faces like masks, fixed always in the expression they wish, consciously or unconsciously, to present to the world. This can be a pleasant smile or an angry growl or a look of sad forbearance or many other looks. Often the mask does show the primary quality of the wearer. A person with a pleasant smile may be a very pleasant person. But he is not only a pleasant person. The mask is an attempt to keep any of his other qualities from showing."

"What do we do to get rid of the masks?" asked Storm.

"The work we are doing will help us lose our masks and allow our faces to become more mobile and expressive. You've seen the changes when you've looked around the circle after class. However, once class is over and we go back into the world again, we have a tendency to put the mask back on."

"But don't we need a mask sometimes?" Bill asked.

"We need at times to control our faces. We never need to have our masks control us.

"June, you wear your mask more tightly than most of us. It rarely slips, even during the class. The fixed smile is getting in the way of your expressing emotions or even feeling them."

"I think I'm a little upset," said June. "I don't like to think of myself as looking like a shark."

"You don't. You aren't showing any teeth. Your lips stay in a slight smile. It's more like saying, 'See what a pleasant person I am. Please don't think badly of me.' "

"That's it!" said June. "That's how I feel most of the time. I don't want people to think badly of me. With my husband, with my daughter, with my friends, it's always the same thing."

"Okay, because your smile is so tightly held, you need to work consciously on letting it go."

"I don't think I even know how."

I went over to June and touched her gently on both cheeks, just above her mouth. "Here, let go right here."

"I don't think I can do it."

"Here."

"Like this?"

June's cheeks and mouth let go slightly. The change in expression was startling. Suddenly, her eyes seemed to come forward in her face and you could see the power and sadness in them. As soon as June felt people looking at her, the smile came back.

"I can't do any more," she said.

"That's enough for now. But that's your homework assignment. Become aware of the muscles that hold your smile in place and let them go any time you notice them holding. I'll work with you as much as I can in class. You may be surprised at what happens.

"I have tried to give you a way of looking at emotions and their discharge as natural and positive, but we have all been subject to years of anti-emotional conditioning. I've had many students in the midst of emotional changes call me up just to get my assurance that they are not going crazy. Let me assure you now: *having emotions does not mean you're going crazy, it means you're going sane.*"

EXERCISES

Let me start by telling you what I said to June: *there is no reason you have to emote.* You may find that the exercises have already begun to churn up emotions for you. You may also find that nothing emotional is happening. This is actually more likely since you are not subject to the emotional stimulation of a class. As long as you are breathing and sounding, you are making progress. Emotions will come when they are ready to.

I must warn you at this point that churning up emotions can be a very scary experience. If the emotions are being stimulated and not actually discharged, the feeling can be very uncomfortable, indeed. In general, your body knows what is good for you and will not allow you to go faster than you are ready to. *Respect your resistances.* If you find these exercises disturbing, I recommend that you do not push yourself to do them, but content yourself for the time being with reading the book and learning in that way. It might also be an occasion for you to seek help through a class or a group or personal therapy.

Emotional Exercises

1) As you are sounding, focus your attention on a person you are close to: a parent, a spouse or lover, a close friend, a boss or superior. Let your feelings for that person mingle with the sound and see what comes out. You may learn things about how you are feeling toward that person at that moment that you didn't know before. Instead of a person, you could let your thoughts go to a specific situation, past or future.

2) Examine your face in the mirror. If you didn't know yourself, what would it tell you? Is there one emotion or thought which seems to be most clearly expressed? What is it? Go through a range of thoughts and memories and see whether your face changes. Is it mobile, or are you mostly stuck in one expression?

Make faces and see how they feel. How do your lips move, your cheeks? Can you move all of your face, or do certain parts seem to be stuck? Consciously try to express different emotions and see how much your face changes. Can you read anger on your face? Sadness? Do you have to exaggerate or is the expression really convincing?

Massage your face, gently and with love. Do this as often as possible, especially any places which seem tight.

Taking It Further

Observe yourself in different real life situations. Are you aware of how you feel? Check this out in emotionally "neutral" situations, like shopping or waiting for a bus, and in emotionally "loaded" situations, like arriving late for work, talking to your parents, arguing with your spouse or lover. What can you feel? What happens to you?

Remember, *feelings are located in the body*. So after you observed what you feel, observe where you feel it. For example, if you feel sad, where do you feel the sadness? In your eyes? Your stomach? If you feel hurt, what sensations in your body correspond to that emotion?

If you are not feeling anything, monitor your breathing. Chances are, you've stopped. Begin to breathe again and see how feelings emerge. Then, examine them. Which emotions move freely for you? Which don't? As you continue the exercises, notice when changes occur.

Once you've observed what you feel, move on to observe what you express. Are the people around you aware of what you feel or do you keep it your secret? Do they see you smiling politely when you are seething inside? Do you want your emotions kept secret or would you be happier letting them out at that moment? If you are not happy with what you discover about your mode of operation, remember that you don't have to change it immediately. Either choice is okay, just be aware it is your choice. *Awareness without judgment is the first step to change.*

How do you handle your anger, sadness, anxiety? Which emotions are okay to show and which aren't? Again, just observe.

Remember, if you notice feelings, you don't immediately have to express them. You can wait till your next sounding to give them vent. If you do feel it would be appropriate to express them at the moment, go ahead.

If you can discharge some of your explosive feelings in private through sounding and reduce their emotional charge, it will be much easier for you to be tactful and reasonable in expressing yourself in public. Many people find that friends and lovers are far more open to expressions of feelings than they thought. Care must be exercised at work, of course. But even there, more leeway might exist than we suspect.

RESULTS

In the following weeks, my students reported some major changes in the way they were dealing with the people around them.

"Two days ago, I got really angry with my

girlfriend." The speaker was Duke. Since throwing his tantrum, his voice had lost some of its breathy quality, and he was a lot easier to hear. "The anger didn't seem that appropriate—I mean, she hadn't done anything that wrong. But she just made me mad.

"So, when I was at my house and my roommate was out, I beat the living hell out of the bed. As I pounded away, I called my girlfriend every name I could think of. I told her I was leaving her, she'd never see me again, and she'd probably not be able to make it without me and die in the gutter."

"How did it work out?" asked Tom.

"Great. After I got through with my tantrum, I just lay on the bed and rested. And feelings of love came to the surface again. I realized how much I cared about her. Usually, when something goes wrong, I can hold a grudge for months. But I feel I got rid of my bad feelings."

"That's terrific," I responded. "Anybody else?"

"I've been saying 'no' all week," June responded. "People are always putting me on committees. This week I refused to take on some new drudge work that came up. My daughter always expects me to chauffeur her everywhere. This week I told her to arrange some other transportation.

"My husband is really used to having his own way and I guess I've always just gone along.

This week I told him about some of the things that bother me about our relationship—things I haven't said for twenty-two years."

"Man, this work is dangerous," said Tom.

"Could you tell us what you said?" asked Storm.

"I told him that I was upset that he never touched me except when he felt sexual."

"Good for you," Storm replied.

"And I told him it upset me when he always brought work home. I wanted him to spend some time just with me."

"How did he react?" Lisa asked.

"He listened. I was afraid he'd just get up and walk out, but he sat there and listened. But he really had trouble understanding. I don't know if it's going to do any good."

"It already has done good," I assured her.

"Has it?" June responded. "I guess it has. I certainly feel better."

"As Tom said, this work is dangerous. As you begin to change, it has to affect those around you. They have to make adjustments."

"What if they can't make adjustments?" asked Storm.

"Then there's trouble," I said. "Students who have gotten in touch with their feelings are far less willing to put up with crap."

"And all this happened because June stopped smiling?" Duke asked.

"It resulted from all the work she has been doing. But the smile was keeping her feelings

from coming to the surface. As she begins to
let it go, as her muscles and breathing patterns
change, she can no longer be satisfied with not
expressing herself."

"I have something to report, also," Bill vol-
unteered. "I had to give a presentation at work
last week. I've spent the last three weeks being
scared. I thought I would get up and just not
be able to say anything. Then I thought I'd
get all the information all bollixed up.

"Well, I gave the presentation and it was
wonderful. I didn't have any trouble remembering. I said it all clearly and forcefully. And
at the end, everyone applauded. I don't know
how that relates to what we do here, but I know
it does."

"I'm really pleased the presentation went
so well," I said. "What we do here is learn to
pay attention to ourselves, to the signals coming from our own bodies. As we do this, we
worry less about other people. Paradoxically,
the more we worry about 'how am I doing,'
the worse we do. You've learned to pay attention to yourself enough to stop worrying and
give a great presentation."

"I'm not sure I understand it," said Bill,
"but it's great."

"Oh, there's one more thing I forgot to say,"
said June. "You know how some of you have
had people notice a change in your faces and
ask if you've changed your hairstyle or lost

weight. Well, I have the best one yet. I met one of my friends for coffee yesterday and she just kept staring at me. Then she asked me, 'Did you have a face lift?' "

6

CHARISMA AND ENERGY FLOW

There are certain people who can walk into a room and soon have all eyes focused on them, without any seeming effort on their part. We describe their special quality as "charisma" or "presence." It is the polar opposite of stage-fright. They are relaxed and confident, fully present in the moment. They don't waste their energy worrying about what other people think of them.

Emotions are one manifestation of the energy which is constantly moving through our bodies. This energy keeps us alive; it powers us. Ancient Chinese medicine views disease as a result of blocked energy in the body. A disease is cured by getting the energy moving again. Freud developed a similar theory of psychological health; all neurosis, he believed, stems from blocked energy.

Developing a full, free energy flow is the fifth step to personal power. Charismatic people seem to radiate energy. In fact, they have more energy than others do. More accurately, they are not blocking their energy, but allowing it to flow through them freely. When I began as an acting teacher, I thought that all I could teach was technique. I felt that charisma was something you couldn't learn—you either had it or you didn't. I was wrong.

You *can* develop charisma. As you breathe more fully and free your body from tension, your energy level increases and you become more expressive. As you learn to sustain and direct a high level of energy flow, you will naturally become charismatic.

The Power in Stillness

By the tenth class, the room sounded like the Bronx Zoo at feeding time. Cries, laughs, and howls filled the air. Duke was still throwing tantrums, which he now concluded by sticking his tongue out and giving the universe a Bronx cheer, which we dubbed the "full-bodied rasberry." Bill had discovered his anger. He pounded the pillows with great ferocity, shrieking his rage. He would pound until he got tired, rest briefly, then start pounding again.

Tom was still laughing. Sometimes his face would contort so that it looked like he was about to cry, but no sound or tears came out. Storm had begun coughing. She would cry, then cough convulsively, then cry again. June, while still not expressing emotion, was making enough noise to share in the general frenzy. Only Lisa was quiet; her sound was almost inaudible, and her only movement was a tiny trembling of her jaw.

I could see that most of the class was reveling in their new emotional freedom. It was a time for me to help them move to the next step. I caught Bill during one of his rest periods. Before he could start pounding again, I told him to keep resting, then I stroked his face gently. "I want you to just lie there, but pay attention to what's happening in your face."

One by one, as each person finished what he or she was doing, I suggested resting and experiencing what was going on in his or her body. I stroked each person gently on the face, chest, or arms, or I just used my hands to move the air several inches above their bodies down from their heads toward their feet. While Duke, June, and Tom began to smile broadly, Bill grimaced with discomfort. I asked him what he felt.

"Little tingles," he replied, irritably. "They're going all over my face."

"Good," I responded. "Stay with them."

After everyone had experienced the new sensations for a while, we formed a circle to discuss what had happened. Bill was still irritated.

"Why did you stop me?" he asked.

"You were only doing half the work. You

were pounding, but you weren't experiencing the results of your pounding."

"What results?" Bill asked.

"The internal results. The good feeling in your body. The tingling which you experienced in your face."

"What about it?" Bill asked, not at all placated.

"When you breathe and sound and emote, as you were all doing before, you actually raise the energy level in your body. I wanted you to experience the sensation of energy flowing."

"Is that what the tingles are? Energy?" asked June.

"Tingling is the sensation many people experience when energy is flowing. Reich called it 'streamings.' At first, it often feels like little prickles, the way your leg might feel after it's fallen asleep. As the body frees up, the sensations get smoother, like being lightly stroked by a piece of silk or a spider's web. Babies have streamings all the time. That's why they are so happy."

"I didn't like the tingles in my face," said Bill. "They felt weird."

"They can be very disconcerting when you're not used to them. In fact, people will go to great lengths to avoid them." I turned to Lisa. "You remember your reaction to the tingles in your hand after the first movement exercise?"

"I really wanted them to go away," said Lisa.

"That was partly because the energy was caught in your hands. It wasn't flowing through the rest of you."

"I felt tingles after you touched me on the arms," said June. "It felt wonderful."

"I always get tingles," said Tom. "I love them."

"You're lucky," I responded.

"Yeah, it's a real trip, man," Tom kidded, embarrassed.

"I still don't understand what's so wonderful about those tingles," Bill said in exasperation.

"They are the feeling of energy flowing. They relate to being fully alive and in the moment."

"I want to ask a question," Duke put in. "Before, when you were touching people, I felt you doing something above me, but I couldn't tell what it was."

"Yeah, I opened my eyes for a minute," said Bill, "and I saw you standing near Duke, waving your arms around. What were you doing?"

"I was moving his aura."

"You were what?"

"Uh-oh," said Tom. "I didn't realize it was going to be one of *those* classes."

What Energy Is

Throughout his career, Wilhelm Reich became more and more fascinated with energy. He actually discovered ways to measure energy flow, recognize energy blockages in the body, and release them so that energy would flow again.

While emoting is part of the freeing process, it is by no means the whole of it. That's an area where many therapists get stuck; they treat emoting as an end in itself and not a step along the path.

Many of my own Reichian sessions would have looked to an outsider as if nothing at all was happening. I would simply lie there, moving energy around my body, and my therapist would sit and watch me.

When I explained this to the group, Tom whistled the theme from "Twilight Zone." Bill looked at me with hurt in his eyes; I had suddenly wiped away ten weeks of understanding and confused him yet again. Conversely, Duke's face softened into a broad smile of understanding.

"I've studied Eastern philosophies and body disciplines for several years," he said. "What you're saying sounds familiar. The concept of centers of energy which power the body is the foundation of Oriental medicine. If the flow of energy is blocked, the Oriental theory goes, we get sick. Acupuncture is designed to help move energy along certain pathways, balancing it throughout the body. T'ai Chi is an exercise form aimed at balancing the body's energy."

"I'm glad you pointed out the connection," I responded. "Reich's great discovery has been known to Eastern philosophies for thousands of years. Sigmund Freud, Reich's mentor, developed a theory analogous to the Eastern belief. He speculated that mental health depends on the free flow of "sexual energy." Any blockage in the flow produces neurosis. Reich took Freud's theory literally and applied it practically. 'If Freud is right,' he said, 'let's find that energy, measure it, discover the physical blockages, and get into the body and free it.'

"Reich did find ways to measure energy flow. He found that energy runs up the back of the body and down the front and that babies experience the tingling sensation of energy flow all the time. As we get older, however, we begin to cut off from the sensations. Tom's ability to experience and enjoy the streamings which characterize energy flow shows an openness which is unusual in our society."

"Gosh," said Tom, in mock embarrassment.

Armoring

"Why do we cut off from the sensations as we get older?" asked June. "Especially if they feel good."

"As children, we find that our feelings often get us into trouble. So we learn to deaden ourselves. We also tighten up to avoid feeling pain. The pathways of energy flow begin to close down. Reich found that people lowered their energy by inhibiting their breathing and/or blocked energy flow by tightening their muscles. He called our tendency to tighten our muscles against energy flow 'armoring.' "

"So as we increase our breathing in class, we're increasing our energy flow," Duke said.

"Exactly. Reich found that while energy flow is vertical, armoring is horizontal. He divided armoring into seven basic segments: the forehead, the jaw, the neck, the chest and arms, the diaphragm, the stomach, and the pelvis and legs."

"Those sound like they correspond to the seven chakras," said Duke.

"What is a chakra?" asked Bill.

"In Eastern thought," said Duke, "there are seven centers of energy in the body, each of which must be freed of blockage on the way to attaining complete freedom or enlightenment. It seems like they're located pretty much where Reich put his seven segments."

"As I said before," I continued, "Reich's theories on energy correspond closely to basic Eastern philosophy. There is an important difference, however. In Eastern thought, you release the lower chakras first, then the upper chakras, moving people away from their bodies and their sexuality toward a sense of oneness with the universe. In Reichian work, the objective is to help people regain the powerful, primitive connection with their bodies that they had as babies."

"Sometimes, after we've been working for a while," said Duke, "I can hardly stand it. I feel like getting up and running around the block. Is that because energy has built up and I don't know how to discharge it?"

"Exactly," I replied. "Strenuous physical activity is clearly one way to discharge energy. Use of the voice is also a way of discharging energy. Many people are uncomfortable with anything near a full energy flow, and they seek to discharge it immediately. That's one of the prime reasons for 'keeping busy'—to keep energy from building."

"But what do we do with all the energy?" asked June.

"Allow it. Let it be. The same as with the breathing and the emotions. It will naturally seek a discharge, whether through seeking out a lover or painting a picture or writing a song or solving a problem. What we are talking about is *creative energy*. If we can let it be, it will cause us to behave creatively. Have you ever noticed how many people who are constantly busy seem to get nothing done?"

There were nods of assent.

"I became powerfully aware of the discrepancy between effort and accomplishment when I was a playwright. I would work on a script for days, sometimes, and not get a single usable line. Other times, I could sit down for an hour and get more written than I had in the previous three days. Somehow, the juices were flowing. I have come to recognize that the creative state results from the build up and free flow of energy."

"But if I'm not doing something, I always feel guilty," said June.

Duke and Storm nodded agreement.

"I know," I responded, "our society has a thing about keeping busy. It's important to realize there is nothing morally righteous about filling up all your time with activities. In fact, it tends to destroy your natural rhythm, the natural build-up and discharge of energy.

"People who are in tune with their natural rhythm, who can allow energy to flow easily through them, have what is called 'charisma' or 'presence.' People gravitate to them."

"Sometimes you see people who seem to have too much energy," said Duke. "You know, they keep doing things, but they still seem to be always bouncing around and talking. You can't be comfortable when they're in the room."

"What you're talking about is quite different from the integrated, flowing energy of the charismatic person. I call it 'manic energy.' It stays almost exclusively in the head and doesn't flow through the rest of the body. You know the expression 'being in your head'? Well, that's what it refers to.

"I know the syndrome because I used to be there. I was a philosophy major in college. I thought I could find all the answers in my head. It took me years to realize how uncomfortable I was. And the reason other people are uncomfortable with someone like that is that he's uncomfortable with himself. He is always trying to 'keep control.'

"Most manic people tend to talk a lot and breathe very little. Talking is one way to discharge energy quickly without letting it go through you. I call it the 'jabber, jabber, jabber syndrome.' Even though energy is discharged, the process is not satisfying because the energy flow has been short-circuited. The energy from the body and the emotions is never allowed to reach the head. I've found with many students that excess verbiage is an attempt to somehow discharge the energy of feelings without expressing the feelings. Of course, it is not very successful.

"Many of the newer transformational groups teach you to change your outlook, change the way you see things. What they teach is very useful, as far as it goes. But the danger is that people put all their energy in their heads, trying to change the way they think. The body doesn't change. There is a manic quality about many 'graduates' of these groups that makes me very uncomfortable. They have changed intellectually, but they have no inner peace."

"You mean, inner peace comes when the energy flows smoothly through your body?" said Tom.

"Exactly," I replied.

The Courage to Surrender

The following week, Tom didn't start his usual laughing and whooping. Instead, he lay very quietly, with only the faintest sound coming out. As I watched, I could see energy moving smoothly through his face, powering the easy sound. After many minutes of easy, almost silent sounding, Tom began to sob quietly. He had watched the women cry and been jealous; he had tried unsuccessfully to get tears to come out; and now, just lying there, he managed to tap into and express his sadness.

I knelt behind him and put my hand under his neck. Gently I lifted up slightly so that his head tilted back a little. This seemed to open up the channel for Tom and the tears came easier. He lay there, gently sobbing. A few tears ran down his cheeks.

Bill had, as usual, launched himself at the pillows. As he pounded with his arms, I told him to bend his knees and lift his pelvis, thrusting down with his pelvis as his arms came down. With this suggestion, Bill's pounding rose to new heights. After a frenzy of pounding, he got tired. This time I didn't have to stop him. He did not resume his activities, but simply lay there, feeling the energy run over him. A beatific smile brightened his face.

After the session, Tom was ecstatic.

"I did it. I cried! Did you hear me? I cried! It was a killer."

"Believe me," said Storm, "crying isn't such a great deal. Sometimes I'm afraid I'll never stop."

"But for Tom it's a breakthrough," I said. "It adds to his emotional repertoire. And did you notice how you did it?" I said to him.

"Yeah," he said. I stopped trying so hard to cry. I just let it happen."

"What was it you did to him?" asked Storm. "It certainly seemed to help him cry."

"I just helped him tilt his head back a little. It is part of what Reich called 'the surrender mechanism.' "

"What's that?" asked Bill.

"When two wolves fight and one wins, the other bears his neck as a signal the fight is over. He actually exposes his most vulnerable spot. Once he does this, the victorious wolf spares him. If he doesn't do it, he will be killed. That is the surrender mechanism."

"But what does that have to do with crying?" asked Bill.

"Surrender to an enemy is only one type of surrender. We can also surrender to a lover or to a feeling. A few weeks ago, I talked about how the body does the same thing in the expression of laughter, tears, and rage. The head goes back, the chest goes down, and the pelvis comes forward. This is the same motion as in orgasm. It is also the motion accompanying every full exhalation of breath. *This is the motion of surrender.* By moving Tom's head back, I helped him surrender more fully to the crying."

"It did help me," said Tom. "Once you did it, I realized that was exactly where my head wanted to go."

"Bill was also able to surrender today."

"I was?" Bill asked.

"After you finished with your pounding, you were able to lie still and allow the energy to flow through you."

"I did. And it felt different. . . It felt good. But I really don't like the word 'surrender,'" Bill continued. "Why can't you just say 'allow.' That doesn't sound quite as bad. 'Surrender' sounds almost un-American."

"I use the word 'surrender' deliberately because it is provocative. There are times, many times, when we need to give up control, to 'surrender.' This is not a negative term. In our society, it takes a great deal of courage to surrender."

The Importance of Anger

"I have something I've been meaning to say," said June, mustering up her courage.

"Go ahead," I encouraged her.

"Well, when Duke and Bill get angry . . . it really upsets me. I know we're supposed to do whatever we want, but when they start pounding and making all that noise, I really don't like it. I wish they would shut up." She tried to soften this last statement with an apologetic smile.

There was tension in the air.

"Bret says that I'm supposed to get angry," Bill responded defensively.

"I know," June answered. It had taken her many weeks to build up the courage to complain. Now she didn't want to back down.

"I can understand how you'd feel that way," I said. "It can be awfully noisy."

"I'll say," June replied.

"How does it make you feel?" I asked.

"It makes me angry."

"So hearing other people express their anger triggers your own anger."

"I guess so."

"Do you think that could be what really bothers you about it? Maybe it's not so much their anger that upsets you as your own."

June sighed. "I guess it's still not okay for me to get angry."

"But do we really have to get angry?" Lisa put in.

"Let me put it this way. I have a friend who believes that he has gone 'beyond' anger. He can see things reasonably, and he doesn't have to get angry. He also can't seem to hold a job, he can hardly afford to pay his rent, and he isn't in a relationship."

"What are you saying?" asked Duke.

"By giving up his anger, he has given up his power. *Anger is a natural manifestation of energy flow.* We need a certain level of aggression to function in life. When we are thwarted, we need to be able to get angry and express it. It's evidence of life energy. I talked before about not being able to surrender. Well, the other side of surrender is the ability to be aggressive and express anger. It is a lot easier to be vulnerable when we know we can defend ourselves if we need to.

"Of course, you all know some people who can get angry easily but don't know how to be hurt or sad. Anger is the only way they can allow energy to flow. Since anger is the only emotion they have access to, it has inordinate power over them. We need the ability to be aggressive and angry, but we also need to be soft, passive, and vulnerable.

"The societal message, however, is never get angry, never surrender, and always be 'reasonable' and polite. In the weeks ahead, we'll see how politeness and 'sweet reason' are often the enemies of real communication."

Pelvic Release

During the following class, I had the students pair up and help each other make sound. I began to work with Storm. Her chest moved smoothly, responding to gentle pressure from my hand. She began to cry. She told me she felt like she was falling apart. I told her not to talk, but just to express the feeling.

A deep sigh came out of her. I encouraged her to keep the sound deep. As her chest moved and she continued to sigh deeply, the sound took on a definite sexual quality. Someone just hearing Storm's sound would have thought that something quite different from a class was happening in my studio.

Her chest lowered further and I could sense the energy going through her stomach into her pelvis. Her expression reflected an intense enjoyment. Then, suddenly, she stiffened. Her eyes opened and she began to scream, "No!" She screamed repeatedly, shaking her head from side to side.

Tom, who had been working with her, tried to comfort Storm, but she pushed him away.

"It's all right," I kept repeating. "It's okay."

Finally she quieted down and just lay there.

"I don't understand it," said Tom. "She seemed to be having such a good time."

"That was the problem," I replied.

Storm looked at us. "Suddenly . . . I don't know . . . I just couldn't take it any more."

"It's okay," I repeated.

"I just got so scared I had to stop."

Even though they had become used to hearing screams, the other students stopped their work and gathered around Storm.

"What happened?" asked June. "Did you get a picture of your childhood? Something terrible that happened?"

"Did you remember someone trying to hurt you?" asked Lisa.

"No. I was feeling really good. Then I got scared. Like something that wasn't supposed to happen was going to happen."

"Like something sexual?" I asked.

"I don't know that I was really feeling sexual," said Storm. "I was just feeling good."

"The two are closely related," I said.

"But then I got scared. It was too much."

"What was?" asked Bill.

"I'm not sure. But it felt like it was going to overwhelm me."

"I saw you get very uncomfortable when energy began to go through your stomach into your pelvis," I said.

"Is that right?" June asked Storm.

"Yes."

June turned to me. "How did you know that?" she asked.

"I don't know how to explain it, but I can see energy moving."

"You can see it?" asked Bill, incredulous.

"What is it you see?" asked June.

"I see a certain aliveness. I guess it's the visual equivalent of the tingles people feel. Maybe I should say I sense it rather than see it, since I can't really describe what I see. And I can see it even through clothing. I only know I'm right because I ask people, and I almost always get confirmation that they felt what I saw."

Tom started whistling the theme from "Twilight Zone" again.

"I believe that anybody can see energy move if they let themselves, just as anybody can move energy once they stop trying to 'control' it with the left brain. As you keep doing this work, you will find yourselves more and more sensitive to the movement of energy in the body."

"Okay," said Tom, "where am I moving energy now?"

"The right side of your face and your right arm."

"How did you know that?" Tom asked. "All I was doing was thinking of the right side of my face and my right arm."

"That's all you have to do to move energy, just think about it. . . . Really, it's not as mysterious as it seems. You remember I said before that the pelvis is the energy center of the body. I talked about a train going a hundred and fifty miles an hour. Well, Storm was starting to feel the train.

"The pelvis is the seat of pleasure and sexuality. As the energy moved down there, Storm got scared. The pelvis is also the center of anger and aggression. Do you remember a couple weeks ago, Bill, when you were pounding and I got you to put your pelvis into it?"

"Yes, it felt much more complete."

"Well, I've been throwing pelvic tantrums for weeks," said Duke.

"Show off," jeered Tom.

"It's from the pelvis that we get our power. People try to look and act powerful by sticking out their chests, but all they do is get in the way of the real power, which comes from the pelvis. When Storm began to tap into that power it scared her."

"What I don't understand," said Storm, "is that it felt so good. Then, all of a sudden. . ."

"It started to feel too good."

"Too good?" Storm looked confused.

"Let's say too intense. That may be easier to understand. I originally got into Reichian therapy because I wanted to be successful, and I was convinced that I had the talent to be. But I knew that my body couldn't stand the intensity of good feelings that being successful would produce. I had done a lot of verbal therapy and come to a good deal of understanding. Now I knew I had to free my body in order to stand the good feelings."

"Isn't that a weird reaction to being successful?" asked Tom.

"Not really. Most of us are afraid to feel too good. We're not built for it. All of this work is ultimately to help us cultivate and enjoy the intense feeling of energy flow that correlates with being fully alive."

EXERCISES

Energy flows through the body and actually surrounds it with what is called an aura. One good way to feel energy is to sit still with your eyes closed and breathe deeply. Then slowly bring your hands together. At some point you will feel a force between the two hands, almost as if it wants to keep them separate. This is one way to sense the body's energy flow.

You can use your exercise sessions to become more aware of the energy which is always flowing through you. After sounding for a while, make it a point to stop and rest. Scan your body and notice any place that is tingling or pulsing. Some areas may feel lighter than or different from the rest. Focus on the area which seems most alive and gradually allow the sensations in that area to enlarge and spread. You may fall asleep during this and that is fine. Add a resting period to your exercises, where you have time to assimilate what you have done. This will help your body get used to a freer and more powerful energy flow.

Jin Shin Do Spine Flow

Jin Shin Do acupressure, a system derived from acupuncture, is designed to keep energy flowing smoothly along certain pathways or "meridian lines" in the body. The idea is to keep all of the organs in the body in balance. Acupressure can work remarkably well to cure the body of illness, and it can give you a very profound and direct sense of energy flowing. Let me provide you with one exercise or "flow," which you can integrate into your exercise routine:

Either sit in a comfortable chair or lie down on the floor. Place one hand on the crown of your head so that your fingers are pointing forward toward your face.

Place two or three fingers of the other hand between the eyebrows, a spot which is called the "third eye." You may feel a pulse in your fingers as they gently keep contact at each spot. If you do, keep both hands in position until the two pulses beat together. If you don't feel a pulse, keep the hands in place until it feels like enough, between two and three minutes.

Once you finish these points, keep the hand on your head and move your other hand to the tip of your nose. Again hold these points for two to three minutes or until it feels like enough or until the pulses synchronize.

Keep up this process, keeping one hand on your head with the fingers pointing forward and moving the other hand as follows:

Place two fingers on the tip of your jaw.

Then in the center of your breastbone, slightly above the nipples.

Then on the solar plexus, directly under the ribs, in the center.

Then on the midpoint of your pubic bone, just above the genitals.

Finally, leave the hand that's on the pubic bone and move the hand that's been on top of your head down to your tailbone.

This is a very subtle exercise and you may
not be aware of exactly what is happening, but
you may feel heat and you may feel tingles. If
you do this exercise a few times over the course
of several days, you may well begin to localize
the sensation of energy moving.

You may do this exercise instead of one of
the Body Awareness exercises before going into
the Voice Visualization and sounding. When
you begin to sound, you may be quite surprised
by how effective this subtle self-touching is.

Taking It Further

Energy flow is an Eastern concept, and many
of the Eastern disciplines are focused specifi-
cally on energy flow. T'ai Chi is a series of
movements designed to balance the body's
energy and is well worth exploring. The theory is that there are two types of energy in the
body—Yang, or masculine, and Yin, or feminine. The movements of T'ai Chi are designed
to balance these two energies.

Yoga involves breathing and exercises
designed to raise the body's energy. Kundalini
Yoga aims at allowing the "Kundalini," or energy,
to rise up the spine.

Classes in T'ai Chi, Yoga, or acupressure
will make you more aware of the energy in
your body and can serve as a useful supple-
ment to this book.

Through the work you have been doing

thus far in conjunction with this book, you have already begun to free yourself and expand your energy field. As you free your energy, you will experience a greater sense of physical and emotional well-being.

RESULTS

During the several weeks that we worked on energy flow, my students reported some important changes in their lives.

Lisa came to class one day radiant. Her usually pale complexion was almost ruddy, and her voice was much louder and more compelling than I had heard it before.

"Is it okay if I speak first today?" she began, unable to contain herself.

"It's okay with me," said Tom. "What about you, Duke?"

"Well, I don't know. . ." Duke began, but Lisa interrupted him.

"My boyfriend and I went for a walk yesterday. He lives up in the Hollywood Hills. I have a problem with my back, which I told Bret about a while ago, and he told me to go for private lessons in Alexander Technique as well as taking the class. My pelvis is—was—retracted and I have scoliosis—that's a curvature of the spine. Usually, we walk around the block and I'm exhausted. Well, this time he asked me if I needed to stop and I said, 'No, let's try a little more.' "

She paused significantly.

"Well, well," Tom put in with exaggerated impatience.

"Well," Lisa said triumphantly, "we walked all the way down to Sunset Boulevard. That was two miles."

"Then he carried you back," Duke put in.

"Then we *walked* all the way back," Lisa corrected him. "And that was uphill."

"That's great," I replied. "Great."

"And it didn't hurt at all," Lisa continued. "I can't believe it." Her smile stretched almost ear to ear. Then she sobered. "I was always afraid I'd be a cripple by the time I was thirty."

"I have some news also," said Bill, seeming surprisingly chastened. "I had the strangest experience the other night. My wife and I were sitting at the dinner table—the kids had gone off—and we were talking. Suddenly she began to tell me things about her childhood, things she had never told me before. She told me about a favorite cousin of hers who had died . . . and a few other things. It made me realize how much she had never told me.

"And then she started to cry. And my wife never cries. I had never heard her cry before. It was amazing. I just watched her for a few minutes. Then I put my arms around her and I held her."

Bill's eyes misted over. "I guess I never really gave her enough room to talk like that before. But since I began to just let the energy flow

through me without trying to do anything . . .
I guess I must have learned how to listen." He
blinked back a few tears and managed a small
smile.

"That's beautiful," Storm responded softly.

"You look so sweet that I really want to give
you a hug," said June. "In fact I think I will,"
and she did.

"Oh, I've got to get in on this too," said
Tom with his usual self-mockery. He went over
and put his arms around both of them.

7

SEX AND PLEASURE: AS MUCH AS YOU CAN STAND

A baby lives for pleasure. It knows what feels good and what doesn't and spends its time seeking the former and avoiding the latter. A healthy baby does not have to look far for pleasure since it can receive sensual gratification from every part of its body. Freud labeled this trait "poly-perverse infantile sexuality," revealing his own attitude toward pleasure.

As we get older, however, we are taught to do what we "should" rather than what feels good. Adults, unlike babies, must balance immediate pleasure with other demands. Unfortunately, most of us have sacrificed too much in order to keep up with what we "should" be doing.

To do what we think we "should," we tighten our muscles and restrict our breathing. Hence, we need stronger and stronger sensations to break through our armor. Drugs and alcohol enjoy such immense popularity in our culture because they allow people to feel free. Many of us need outside help to break down the barriers separating us from our own joy and spontaneity.

Increasing your capacity for joy and pleasure is the sixth step to personal power. Through the work described in this book, you can rediscover and reintegrate pleasure into your daily life.

Surrender to Pleasure

It was late fall and I had begun to turn on the heaters against the chill in the Los Angeles air. The electric heaters gave a warm glow to the darkened room. My students were lying on the floor, sounding. During the past few weeks, Duke had moved out of the tantrum stage and had begun to sound more quietly. This time he was so silent that I could hear almost no sound. And yet there was an intensity, a sense of deep peace about him.

I came over to him. As soon as he felt my presence, he opened his eyes. "You know, it's strange . . ." he began.

"Don't talk now," I returned. "Close your eyes again."

He did and I knelt beside him, placing my hand near his forehead with my palm facing down, helping the energy move through his eyes, where I could sense a blockage. Duke's breathing got deeper and his body filled with energy. He was glowing almost as much as the heater. His face stretched into a beatific grin.

When the sounding was over, Duke got up slowly and joined the circle. He was smiling so broadly and radiating so much energy that everybody stared at him. "That was really something," he said, coming back slowly.

"What happened?" June asked.

"I don't really know. I've never felt like that. I felt like I was melting. I felt so good and so peaceful. But, you know, it felt scary. I mean, my mind kept trying to get me to worry about this or that. I felt your hand above my eyes, Bret, and I felt how it completed the energy flow. And it was hard to surrender to all the pleasure. I think I could really feel what you were going through, Storm."

"But *you* let it happen," said Storm, clearly dissatisfied with herself.

"You will too," I assured her.

"When?" she asked.

"Soon," I responded.

"But I want to let it happen now."

"Why do we have so much resistance to feeling pleasure?" June asked.

"Well, for one thing," I responded, "we're not used to it. As with emotions, we've tightened up so that our bodies have trouble handling it. The feeling is too intense. And society really promotes this kind of denial—don't feel too good. Many of us are afraid that if we're too happy, it might be taken away."

"It doesn't feel very philosophical, just 'feeling good,'" said Duke. "I mean it doesn't feel very deep. I always thought only superficial people could feel good because they didn't realize the mess the world was in . . . I guess I'm getting more and more superficial," he said as he lay luxuriously back on the floor.

"But isn't there something wrong with all this?" asked Bill. "I mean we can't just lie around feeling good. What would happen to the world?"

"It would probably be in a lot better shape than it is now," Tom replied.

Pleasure and Sexuality

Storm got her opportunity to surrender to pleasure two classes later. During the sounding, she was unusually quiet. I walked up to her and she opened her eyes.

"I'm embarrassed," she said.

"About what?" I asked.

"Oh, you know. It's all those feelings all over . . . I'm . . . I'm afraid I'm going to, you know . . . have an orgasm."

Storm, who was able to scream at the top of her lungs, cry and pound in front of the class, was embarrassed that we might see her feel good.

I explained to her that she would most likely not have the screaming orgasm she wished-feared, but rather a subtle and gentle sensation of pleasurable tingles all over her body, going down her legs.

"You mean," she said, "I'm thinking of having an orgasm because that's the only way I know of experiencing pleasure."

"Exactly. I'm all for better orgasms. In fact, this work definitely helps that happen. Reich's original goal was to help people have better orgasms. But the feelings you're having are like those of a baby. They could be easily changed into something else, but you're quite safe for now."

"So what should I do?" asked Storm.

"Lie back and enjoy the feelings," I responded.

As Storm lay back, a blissful, childlike smile on her face, I saw Lisa begin to move her legs, as if she was running away from something. As I watched, she began swaying her pelvis from side to side, as if her lower body were saying "no."

I walked over to her and stopped the swaying motion of her legs. Then I told her to lift her pelvis straight up in the air and let it come straight down. She did this only once, then stopped. "Keep going," I urged. The second time Lisa lifted her pelvis, she began crying. She cried softly and deeply for a long time. After a while, the tears subsided.

"How do you feel?" I asked her.

"Peaceful."

"Where do you feel peaceful?"

"Down there." She indicated her lower abdomen and her groin.

We were both silent for a while in the midst of the noise around us. Then she smiled, a smile which she quickly suppressed, as if she had done something wrong.

"What were you smiling about?"

"Nothing."

Silence again.

"I was just thinking that it might be nice to touch myself down there now."

"It didn't used to be nice?"

"No. My parents were down on that. All through my childhood. They made me feel dirty. I've never been able to really enjoy sex. I mean, it can be pretty good sometimes, but there's always something in the way. And whenever I touch myself, I do it because I have to, never just because I enjoy it."

"Maybe you can start enjoying it now."

"Maybe I can."

Later that evening, with Lisa's and Storm's permission, I brought up what had happened in our discussion circle.

"It really embarrasses me to talk about touching myself sexually in front of other people," Lisa said.

"It really embarrasses me, too," I responded. "How many of you find this discussion a little embarrassing?"

"Not me, man," said Tom. "I want to hear

more, more!" But he raised his hand sheepishly, along with everybody else.

"It's characteristic of our society," I continued. "Growing up in our culture, I would be tempted to say that there would be something wrong with us if we didn't find talking about sex embarrassing. Yet there are societies, as Margaret Mead writes about in *Coming of Age in Samoa*, where sexuality is a natural, integrated part of life."

"It's funny though," said Duke, "because the movies and even television are always hinting at sexual acts and even showing them. Sex sells."

"We are a sex-obsessed culture," I said. "We are fascinated by sexuality, even though there is something about it that still makes us uncomfortable. That is because we see sexuality not as a natural part of life, but as a separate entity, not integrated into our way of living.

"Because we have cut ourselves off from experiencing pleasure in the variety of ways it is meant to be experienced, we place an inordinate burden on sexuality. We use it for—and confuse it with—many other sensations and emotions."

"Like what?" asked Bill.

"Just experiencing the streaming sensations, as Storm did before, affection, being touched, getting to know someone else. We can explore a whole range of sensuality without necessarily having to get sexual. One of the wonderful things that happens in this class is that people get a chance to experience a whole range of possible relationships. And, while we are helping each other, we get to touch each other.

"Reich believed that when you deny people sexual pleasure you deny them a real sense of what good feelings are. They behave more and more on 'shoulds,' on what they think they have to do. He saw sexual liberation as part of social liberation. Good, happy sex keeps us from armoring."

"But you don't mean that the class is going to make us promiscuous?" said June.

"Oh, wow," Tom responded.

"Seriously," June went on. "This talk makes me uncomfortable. And I have been feeling more sexual lately and it makes me nervous. I'm afraid I may do something that isn't right."

"You're raising a very important issue," I said. "What do we do with all this new pleasurable energy? As I said, there is a whole range of affectionate and sensual contact possible as your body becomes looser. As your body can handle more pleasurable energy, there is less driving need for discharge through sex.

"When Reich talked about orgasm, he was talking about a total discharge that involved the entire body. He believed, and I do too, that as you become more orgasmic, it is natural to seek pleasure in the context of a long-term, loving relationship."

"Why is that?" asked Tom.

"A full orgasm is a surrender of conscious control, which is hard to do in a casual relationship. There are too many inhibitions. You remember, we talked a few weeks ago about keeping energy in the head and discharging through talking. Well, recreational sex is the same phenomenon, but at the other end of the body. Energy builds and discharges in the genitals. There is not the build, flow, and discharge of the total energy of the body. Sexuality that involves the heart as well as the genitals is far more satisfying."

"Since we've started this work, I've become a lot more sexual," said Duke. "My girlfriend is very pleased."

"One of the benefits of this work, which I don't feel comfortable advertising, is that it improves your sex life."

Bill tightened his jaw, as he did when he was troubled. "This is a little embarrassing for me to talk about. But since I started this work, I haven't been as sexual. I mean, sometimes I don't feel like doing anything."

"Is that new for you?" I asked.

Bill looked around the room and decided to go ahead. "Before, I was always looking. And my wife and I would make love three times a week like clockwork. I was always ready. Now, I just don't want to do it all the time."

"How do you feel about that?" I asked.

"Well, I feel funny. I mean, I'm afraid there

might be something wrong with me."

"How does your body feel?"

"That's the funny part. I actually feel relieved. It's like I was putting on a show and now I don't have to anymore. I don't feel like I have to prove anything."

"How is your wife taking it?"

"I was afraid she might be really upset, but she isn't. She seems relieved too."

"Well, we have sex for all kinds of reasons, not just for pleasure. It sounds like you're balancing out. You're dropping the need to prove yourself. On an energy level, if you are more relaxed and able to discharge energy elsewhere, you don't need to have sex all the time. As I loosened up through this work, my orgasms lost a certain desperate intensity because, before, having an orgasm was the only way I could turn off the constant 'click, click, clicking' of my left brain. I know when I got occupied with building my business and putting energy out to a lot of people, I didn't want to make love for weeks at a time. I was worried about how my lady would take it, but it was actually a very peaceful feeling. I didn't feel so driven. . . When you make love, how is it?" I asked Bill.

"It's wonderful. It's better than it's ever been. I'm able to have a much fuller orgasm—to let go easier."

"So you feel good about it?"

"I really do. I guess I just have to adjust my image from a man who walks around hard all the time. It's really nice to give that up."

"You seem softer, more gentle," said June. "Your eyes are changing."

Bill smiled, embarrassed. "I'm still not used to it, but I really like it. . . . Sometimes now my wife and I will just lie there and touch each other gently, and it doesn't have to lead to sex."

Your sexuality is a mirror of how you relate to people. As you become more open and vulnerable, your ability to experience orgasm will increase. Orgasm is the ultimate giving up of control—the ultimate surrender.

The Joy of Eating

"Besides feeling more sexual," said June, "there's something else making me nervous. I've been eating more."

"You still look nice and slim to me," said Lisa. (June was indeed quite slender.)

"I know," June replied with some worry, "but I always have a constant battle with food. Two days ago I broke down and had a chocolate malted."

"Oh my God!" cried Tom in mock dismay.

"You don't understand. Once I get started, it's almost impossible to stop myself."

"Did you have a chocolate malted yesterday?" I asked her.

"No."

"Today?"

"No," June replied.

"You see what I'm getting at. You've eaten a chocolate malted, but your sweet tooth hasn't taken over."

"But it might!" June protested.

"Eating is designed to be pleasurable. In fact, taking in food is our first taste of pleasure. Our culture has managed to turn it into a constant battle for many of us."

"But what if eating is too pleasurable?" June asked. "If I let myself just eat for the pleasure of it, I'd be as fat as a house."

"I know what you mean," said Storm.

"I don't think that's necessarily true," I replied. "They've done studies that show that young children, eating for pleasure, will naturally eat a healthy, balanced diet. Overeaters Anonymous suggests that most people who overeat constantly do not do so because it is pleasurable. Often they are trying to stuff down feelings. Often eating and love have gotten mixed up in childhood, and the eating disorders correlate with the way we are fed and loved as children."

"I can relate to that," said Storm.

"So can I," June added.

"Our society also has an obsession with thinness that is quite unique in history. If you look at old paintings, or even old Tarzan movies, you will see how the standard of beauty has changed."

"Are you saying that people today are trying to be too thin?" asked Bill.

"Basically, yes. And in our obsession with weight, we have turned eating, one of our most pleasurable activities, into a test of will, a moral struggle. People get hung up on eating as another 'should.' You've all heard people judging themselves by what they eat: 'I was good today, I didn't have any sweets.' 'I was bad today, I had a hot dog.' People into health food also fall into that trap.

"We really don't need to be hard on ourselves. *The problem of eating recedes into the background if you gear your life around pleasure and then make sure there is enough pleasure in your life.*

"I had one student who really used to put herself down as a compulsive eater. She was thin as a rail, but she felt like she couldn't stop eating. She would binge, then heap abuse on herself. I told her that the next time she pigged out, she shouldn't censor herself, but rather look at herself in amazement. 'Boy, did I pig out. I bet nobody else could pig out as well as that.'"

There was some laughter.

"In that way, I got her to take eating out of the realm of struggle and to stop using food as an excuse for self-abuse. I'm not saying you're doing that, but a chocolate malted once in a while never hurt anyone. In fact, it's probably really good for you."

"What do you mean, good for you?" asked Bill. "It's got all kinds of fat and sugar in it."

"That may be true, but the pleasure and

the nurturing are good for the soul."

"Are you suggesting that we should drink chocolate malteds whenever we want?" Storm asked. "Because I do have a weight problem . . ."

"I'm suggesting occasional chocolate malts, a balanced diet of food, a balanced diet of pleasure, and getting eating out of the realm of battle, worry, and moral judgment."

June's face lit up in a smile. "That sounds good to me. Actually, I'm pretty sick of getting on myself . . . If I get fat now and my husband throws me out, it'll be your fault," she warned.

"I'll take the chance," I replied.

The Need to Play

The following class, Lisa again lay on the floor quietly, her jaw quivering. I began to massage deeply the area around her eyes and nose. Her face tightened in response to my fingers. I stopped rubbing and told her to keep up the motion. Lisa tightened her face into what was clearly a sneer, then let it go. As she kept doing this, she began to make a sneering sound through her nose.

"Nyaah," she said. "Nyaah." Then she stuck her tongue way out of her mouth. "Nyaah," she shouted. Then she pulled her tongue back and began to giggle wickedly, as if she'd gotten away with something.

"Go ahead," I urged her.

Again the sneer, again the tongue came

out, again the wicked giggle. Lisa kept sticking her tongue out and each time her laughter grew until she ended in a paroxysm of giggling. Her whole body moved and rocked with joyful laughter.

When we gathered in our circle later, Tom asked her what she was giggling about.

"This is a serious class, you know," he said, with mock irritation.

"I was sticking my tongue out," Lisa responded. "And then I would realize that I shouldn't be doing it, it wasn't polite, so I would start to giggle. Then I would do it again. It was wonderful."

"You look wonderful," I said. "Your face has much more color than usual. You look very animated, very alive. That's one of the ways you can tell an increase in energy. When an area is blocked, it tends to look whitish; when energy is flowing, circulation improves and the color reddens."

"You mean a drunk has a red nose because of energy?" asked Tom.

"In that case, the energy is blocked there. Too much accumulates. That's what happens when someone blushes."

"I feel like blushing," said Lisa.

"Why?" I asked.

"I'm embarrassed for being so silly."

"Being silly is one of our greatest needs," I responded. "You were expressing yourself through play, the way we are designed to."

"That's okay when we're children," Bill said. "But aren't we supposed to be different as adults?"

"My guess is that Lisa never got to do anywhere near enough playing as a child," I replied.

"That's true," Lisa responded. "I never felt I could be silly and disrespectful. Even as a baby, my relatives told me I was always very serious."

"You got the message early," I replied.

"Are you saying that we all really need to stick out our tongues and go 'Nyaah' like that?" Bill asked.

"Absolutely," I responded.

"You especially, Bill," Tom put in.

"Not me," Bill shot back.

"I can understand that, Bill," said Duke. "You're a serious guy."

"I am," said Bill with some pride.

"You know," said June, "I think Bill's probably more afraid of being silly than he is of screaming or crying."

"That's probably true," Bill said thoughtfully.

"That reminds me of one of the people I've been seeing privately," I said. "He's a psychotherapist and he was really into the dirty business of getting his emotions out.

"The psychotherapist usually felt he needed to cry, so he would carefully set a box of tissues beside him before he lay on the mat. I had the roughest time getting him to do what his body wanted to do rather than what he *thought* it wanted to do.

"He would start out trying to cry. His belly would ripple with his attempt to sob, but nothing much would happen. Gradually, by encouraging him and touching his face gently, I got him to allow the quivering in his belly to spread. Soon his whole body began shaking violently.

" 'It's fear,' he said as he was shaking. 'I'm experiencing fear.'

" 'Just let yourself keep shaking,' I responded.

"But he couldn't stand it anymore and he sat up.

"The next session, the same thing happened. This time I got him to go with the shaking longer, and it began to calm down. His body began to move easily in a rhythm, like a baby playing in a crib. His head, however, was still shaking violently back and forth, saying 'no.'

"I had him sit up and I demonstrated what his body was doing, leaving out the negative motion of the head.

" 'It looks like a baby,' he said.

" 'And what's the baby doing?'

" 'Throwing a tantrum?'

" 'Does that really look like a tantrum to you? It's pretty peaceful for a tantrum.'

"He still didn't get it, and I didn't tell him. The third session, however, I got him into the shaking, which calmed down into easy, gentle, babylike rocking. He opened his eyes, looked at me and began to laugh—a deep, rich, powerful laugh. 'I know what I'm doing,' he said. 'I'm potchkying.' "

"What's potchkying?" asked Tom, interrupting my narrative.

"Playing," Bill replied.

" 'Potchky, potchky, potchky,' the serious therapist said happily, playing like a baby, laughing.

"It took him several times going through the experience before he began to see the value. Here he was, used to therapy as a heavy, painful experience, but he had gone through the heavy, painful part. What he needed was to play. He was spending his life forcing himself to be serious.

"This man's 'problem' as he saw it was that he felt dependent on women and tied to his mother. It became clear why he couldn't play: playing would be a way of giving himself pleasure and breaking his dependency. He was always looking outside for pleasure and satisfaction. His guilt stopped him from playing and enjoying himself. His mother was so miserable, how could he have the nerve to be happy?

"I told him that his greatest task was to let himself feel pleasure as often as possible. We had several more sessions. Each time I would take him through whatever surface emotion he was feeling to the childish pleasure underneath. When he first came to me, he used to wake up every morning shaking—from fear, he assumed. Now he would put on music, let the shaking slow down, and potchky to his heart's content. What he was afraid of was the pleasure he could feel. He decided I should rename my method 'the potchky school of therapy.' "

"That's a great story," said Storm, laughing when I had finished.

"That shaking you talked about," said Duke. "Wasn't that energy flow?"

"Yes, it was. As the psychotherapist relaxed and breathed, the energy built up in his body. Because his body was not free enough to let it pass through easily, he began the violent shaking. Once he could potchky, he could let the energy move smoothly. *Playing is moving energy pleasurably. It is vitally important in keeping us healthy and in condition.*"

"But there's a real difference between Lisa's playing and that guy's playing," said Tom. "The guy's playing was self-contained and showed self-sufficiency. Lisa's playing was a sign of lack of respect."

"Good observation," I responded. "Lisa was actually reaching out her tongue in a way our society disapproves of violently. But even though she was being disrespectful, she was still reaching out. We'll be getting into that more in the next few weeks."

Living For Pleasure

I'm still not comfortable with all this emphasis on pleasure," Bill said. "If people just lived for pleasure, I'm just not sure anyone would ever get anything done."

"That was Freud's theory," I responded. "He figured that if we didn't all have neuroses, we would spend our lives sitting under palm trees. But the fact is that children are always exploring, learning, discovering, and creating because it feels good. There is a natural human drive to move, to act, to do. Take our school system. Children learn more for the sheer joy of learning and discovery than they ever do when they are told to learn something. I'll never forget how I used to love poetry until I was forced to read a very, very long poem called *Evangeline*. I could never feel the same about poetry after that."

"I was the same way with school," said June. "I used to love art until the third grade, when they taught me how to draw a house. That finished me."

"Hey, I don't know, guys," Tom responded. "I sure wouldn't be able to do my work in school if I didn't force myself."

"If it isn't enjoyable, why are you going?" asked Storm.

"I really want to get a degree," Tom replied.

"Of course he does," said Bill. "There are some things you do because they pay off later.

There are some days my job drives me crazy, but I keep at it."

"But overall," I asked, "do you like what you're doing?"

"Yes, I do. And I love being in business for myself. Even if it's hard sometimes."

"I remember when I quit one job," said Storm, "and I told my boss it was because I didn't like it. He couldn't believe it. 'Why should you enjoy your job?' he asked me, dumbfounded. 'I don't enjoy my job. I don't know anybody who enjoys their job. But look at how much money you're making.' "

"The trouble comes when we lose the ability to feel pleasure." I said. "As babies, we base our decisions on what feels good. As we get older, and life becomes more complicated, we start to modify the pleasure principle by what Freud called the 'reality principle.' "

"What's that?" Storm asked.

"You know how kids can embarrass their parents. Uncle Harry comes to visit and he's overweight and the kid says, 'Boy, you sure are fat, Uncle Harry.' Well, at some point, the kid learns that he isn't supposed to say that, either because he gets in trouble or because he likes Uncle Harry and doesn't want to hurt his feelings. Similarly, he learns that if he acts like a baby, he may be denied some grown-up privileges, and if he eats his cookie now, he won't have it for later. In other words, he makes choices, sometimes postponing pleasure which may result in pain later. That's what Freud called the 'reality principle.'

"Ideally, as we grow up, we come to a healthy balance between pleasure and responsibility to others. We still get pleasure, but in a socially modified and adult form. Unfortunately, this rarely happens. Instead, the two are compartmentalized, with the overwhelming majority of time allotted to what seems to be the reality principle in order to support an occasional pleasure binge. In fact, most of us have subordinated both pleasure and reality principles to 'shoulds.' We do what our parents or society tell us we ought to be doing.

"You know you're operating on 'shoulds' if you feel that you have no choice, that you have to do what you're doing."

"I know that feeling," said June.

"You can see this syndrome time and again," I said, "with people stuck in boring jobs or putting up with obnoxious friends and relatives.

"As you continue this work, you will find that the pleasure principle more and more assumes its rightful place in your life. The need for pleasure is a natural need, which begins to assert itself as your body loosens up. Pleasure feels so good that you begin to seek it out more and more in your daily life. You become much clearer about people and situations you like and dislike, and you'll find yourself seeking out the former and avoiding the latter. You move away from the 'shoulds' and start going for what you want."

"You mean you stop being satisfied with being a cog in the wheel?" asked Tom.

"Exactly."

"You know," Tom mused, "this work is really subversive. It's subtle, but it's subversive."

"In this country, feeling pleasure can be a subversive activity."

"But what about responsibilities?" Bill demanded. "What about other people?"

"Remember how much more helpful you can be to someone else during the sounding when you're breathing and comfortable. It's the same thing in life. *You can do a lot more for other people through the pleasure it gives you than you can because you should.*"

EXERCISES

We are designed to feel pleasure almost all the time. The simple acts of everyday living—moving, speaking, and breathing—are all essentially pleasurable. Pleasure is always felt in the body. I would like you to take this opportunity to tune into the pleasure of your senses. You can use this book as an excuse to indulge yourself.

Filling Your Senses

Listen to a beautiful piece of music and observe what happens in your body. You may feel the tingling sensations I described in the previous chapter. Notice where you feel them. I often get tingles up and down my spine when I listen to music.

Please your other senses. Go for a walk someplace beautiful. Concentrate first on what you see, then on what you smell. Again, notice how the pleasure manifests itself in your body.

To explore touch, it would help if you have a partner—someone willing, even eager, to be nice to you. Have your partner lightly stroke you with a feather or a soft piece of silk. Lie on your back and let the stroking go down your body. Notice how different parts of your body respond differently, which parts give you the most pleasure.

Also try lying on your stomach and having the stroking go down your back and legs. See how differently the two experiences feel.

Eating is one of our most highly charged activities. Eat something you thoroughly enjoy. Eat it slowly and notice the different sensations: first, the smell of each bite, how it reaches you, then the tactile sensations of your teeth, lips, and tongue. Even notice the sensation as the food goes down your throat. See if you can follow the sensation all the way down into your stomach. Appreciate how much pleasure you can give yourself through simple awareness of this experience.

Taking It Further

Start noticing your body in different situations, as you did with breathing and emotions. This time notice which people and situations give you pleasure. What does your body feel like? *Pleasure is always a bodily sensation. Notice where in your body you feel it.*

Notice when you deny yourself pleasure. Are there certain people with whom you allow yourself pleasure, others with whom you deny yourself? Does your breathing decrease when you deny yourself pleasure? Notice what happens to your body and breathing at such times.

You have a natural, inborn right to pleasure. As you continue to do this work, you will find yourself seeking out more people and situations which give you pleasure and avoiding those which don't.

RESULTS

The following week, Tom came in to class looking unusually serious.

"I want to tell you guys something, and it's kind of hard for me, so nobody interrupt, okay?" He looked around the room cautiously. "You see, I don't like to talk about this, but the last few years, I've been something of a pothead."

Duke and Storm chortled.

"Hey, you guys, I'm serious," Tom hushed them up. "I used to do a lot of weed. I really like to get a buzz on. I'd try to cut down, but I'd go to parties and everybody would be smoking. There's a lot of pressure. Besides, it feels *so good*. I almost flunked out of school last quarter because of it, but I just couldn't lick it.

"Well, since I've been doing this class, I've gotten into how good it feels just to *breathe*, and feel the energy *flow*. Damn, I always get tingles. Well, it feels as good as the drugs. I mean, I wouldn't have believed it if someone had told me, but it does."

"Amazing, isn't it?" I remarked. I could see Duke nodding affirmatively.

"So with all the breathing," Tom continued, "I've been able to cut down the drugs to a minimum. People look at me funny at parties. So what? I mean, I know something they don't even suspect. Air, man. That's the best drug there is.

"Sure, drugs feel good. But what kind of pleasure is that when you're sick the next day and you never get anything done? *Breathing, that's the real high.*"

Tom broke into his usual grin. "It's like they say in the ad. It feels good and it's good for you, too."

We all grinned back at him.

"You know," said Duke, "I read in the paper that they've recently discovered that the brain can produce a morphinelike substance that produces a natural high. That's what they think 'runner's high' really is. I wonder if Tom is talking about the same thing."

"I think he is," I responded. "I've had several long distance runners take my class, all of whom said they got a feeling of euphoria from the breathing that was just like the high they got while running. My feeling is that it's the breathing which triggers the chemical reaction in the brain."

Storm had come into class glowing. There was an embarrassed flush to her cheeks. "Well, it finally happened," she announced. "I finally met a guy. I haven't really been seeing anyone for almost a year, since I broke up with my last boyfriend. But I met this guy, and I've been seeing him every night this week. I don't quite believe it, but it's happening."

"That's great, that's really great," said June.

"I wonder why you suddenly met somebody after such a long time," I said ironically.

"You think it has something to do with the class?" Storm asked, all innocence.

"I think it might. You give the world the signal and things begin to happen."

"A lot happens when you surrender to pleasure, doesn't it?" commented Lisa.

"It certainly does," I replied.

8

LOVING AND FIGHTING: PATHS TO INTIMACY

Perhaps more than anything else in life, we all crave love and friendship. Yet we are often afraid to reach out for it. We are built to function with others on every level, from convenience to deepest intimacy. Yet lack of satisfying intimacy and connection with others is all too common in our culture.

For many, a pattern starts in childhood: we reach out and do not get what we want. We are even blamed or hurt for asking. As we learn that reaching out is useless, or even dangerous, we stop reaching.

Since reaching out is natural, we begin literally to hold ourselves back. The muscles around the chest harden to protect the heart. Shoulder and neck muscles tighten to keep us from giving in to our need. As with the arms, our voices also lose their ability to express how we feel so that we can connect with other people.

As adults, we need to overcome our fears and reown our natural impulse to reach out. Improving our ability to reach out to other people and achieve intimacy is the seventh step to personal power. We reach out to others through loving and through fighting—ways of connecting which are interrelated. The discharge of anger can be an essential step in the ability to love.

Letting Go of Pride

"I think I finally understand what this class is really about." The speaker was Duke. It was the first class of the new year and we were all happy to be back together after a three-week hiatus. Eyes were bright, faces glowing. Obviously, a lot had happened during the three weeks. Duke's eyes were large and there was a new look in them, a look of softness and of wonder.

"During the vacation, I had a difficult experience. My girlfriend told me that she had slept with someone else."

The silence which surrounded Duke suddenly deepened.

"We were in bed together and we were arguing about sex and she just came out and told me."

"It must have been a shock," said Tom.

"It was. My first impulse was to hit her, and

I almost did. But I stopped myself. Then I got up and started putting on my clothes. She was pleading with me to listen to her, but I just wanted to get the hell out of there. Then, I noticed what my body was doing. My chest was raised, my shoulders were tightened and pulled together. And of course I had stopped breathing.

"I felt my body—nothing moving, everything tensed—and I realized that I just couldn't stand being that uncomfortable. So I just let go. And when I stopped holding my body and started breathing again, everything changed. Suddenly, I felt like I was wounded and needed to be comforted. Instead of seeing my girlfriend from a great distance, I felt her pain. So, instead of storming out like I usually did when I got angry, I stayed."

"It must have been very hard for you," Storm said sympathetically.

"It was strange. My pride was really hurt, that was the main thing. I was going to storm out and 'show her.' But when I let my body go, it all changed. I just did *what I really wanted to do, not what I thought I wanted*. I was all hung up on how bad it looked, how embarrassing it was. But when I started breathing, I tuned into how I felt. And there was such a relief in dropping that big, brave act I liked to put on."

"I think that staying with her was very brave," responded June.

"It didn't feel brave. It just felt peaceful

and right, like what I really wanted to do."

"What happened?" asked Tom.

"She told me she had been feeling bad about her own sexuality. She felt that I felt she wasn't orgasmic enough. And she went and saw an old boyfriend because she needed to prove herself. I sulked, she held me, and we both cried."

"Are you still seeing each other?" asked Bill.

"That's the really amazing part. I felt closer to her than I ever have."

"How can that be?" Bill asked. "After what happened?"

"A fight like that either breaks you up or it brings you closer together," answered Storm.

"That's right," said Duke. "It's like there was always a barrier between us that isn't there anymore."

"I don't think I want the class to make me that forgiving," said Bill.

"The class didn't make me do anything," Duke replied. "I just learned to let go of my pride and feel what I really felt. I could have kept my breath held and my muscles tight and stormed out. The class gave me a choice. Before, my breathing was always constricted and my muscles were always tense. I was always ready to withdraw. There wouldn't have been any change to notice."

I was grinning like a Cheshire cat. Duke had fully understood and utilized the work we had been doing together for six months. He was able to let his body show him what he really wanted to do.

At first, he had followed his old pattern and stopped breathing in order not to feel the pain. He had raised his chest to put back his wounded pride. He had pulled back his shoulders to avoid reaching out. In that position or posture, he really had no choice but to storm out. There was no way he could make contact with another person.

When he changed his body pattern, he was not only able to feel the deeper emotions buried under his defensive stance, but he could allow his feelings to motivate his actions. He was able to discover and go after what he *really* wanted, rather than what he *thought* he wanted. He moved past worrying about how things *looked* to tuning into how they *felt*.

Bill's response to Duke's story was the expected one. "I would have stormed out," he said.

"That would have been perfectly fine," I responded, "if that was your impulse. Perhaps the impulse would be to stand up and scream at her. I'm not saying that Duke's behavior was *right* behavior; that would just be another 'should.' All I'm saying is that it was right for him at the time."

"But what if he hauled off and slugged her?" asked Tom. "He said that was his first impulse."

"Good question. First of all, I do not advocate violence. Yelling and screaming, yes. Violence, no. We always have to be aware of a reality principle which works in conjunction with the pleasure principle. When you hit someone else, you could hurt them, you could injure them. Duke, being a big guy, has to be particularly aware of this. Secondly, hitting someone is an ineffective way of reaching out."

"What do you mean?" asked Bill.

"There really isn't that much difference between this [I reached out threateningly toward Bill with closed firsts; he instinctively drew back] and this [I opened my fists and reached out gently with my open hands]. Both are ways of reaching out. Many times, people are afraid to reach out with open hands, so they reach out with their fists instead. This is what we see in the behavior of juvenile delinquents. Fighting is the only way they know to make contact.

"When I was a camp counselor many years ago, the boy campers felt they were too big to be hugged, so they would provoke me until I hit them. To them it seemed the only permissible form of contact. I was young then, and it took me quite a while to figure out what was going on and touch them lovingly instead."

There was some silence when I finished. I could see June and Lisa nodding their heads in agreement.

"What Duke's behavior shows us is that you can act on your pride and feel virtuous and superior or you can act on what you feel and get your needs met. Very often, what feels good is to reach out to another person rather than withdraw."

"But what if you reach out to someone else," Storm asked, "and then you hate yourself in the morning?"

There was general sniggering.

"You learn the difference between momentary pleasure and long-range pleasure," I responded. "If a certain impulse always leads to long-range disaster, you learn not to act on that impulse."

Dropping Your Act

"I have something I want to report also," announced Tom. "My parents used to fight all the time when I was young. It was really vicious. But I didn't let myself get affected by it. I was hiding somewhere in this sturdy, unemotional thirteen-year-old. I never cried or anything like that. That's when I started smoking dope all the time. So I could be detached.

"Well, yesterday my parents started in again and I listened for a little, then I went off into my room like I usually do. But then something different happened. I didn't want to smoke dope—I told you I'm not using it much anymore. So I just sat there. And then I started to cry. Really. The tears just streamed down my cheeks.

"Then, before I knew it, I was back in the living room yelling at my parents. I let them both have it. I told them exactly how lame they both were and how much it hurt me to see them fighting all the time. My mom told me It was sounding like my dad and my dad told me I was sounding like my mom and that was funny. But I told them that I was me and I was hurting and I cried and cried and it felt good. I felt really good."

Tom beamed. He looked as if a weight had been lifted off his shoulders, and a joyous energy seemed to radiate from his whole body.

"I feel so good!" he shouted.

"Congratulations," said Duke.

"It's so great not trying to be cool all the time," said Tom.

"I wish I could tell my parents when they get to me," said Lisa.

"You will," I assured her.

"You know, the amazing part," said Tom, "the next day my dad apologized to *me*. And he told me that he loved me. He'd never done that before. Next, I think I'm going to try hugging him," Tom continued, grinning mischievously. "I wonder how he'll deal with that."

I was very pleased. I remembered how much Tom had wanted to cry in class and how hard it was for him. All those years of being cool and detached. I remembered how good he felt when he finally could cry in class. He had relearned a very useful skill.

"I feel much closer to my parents than I have in years," Tom said.

"That's because you stood your ground," I replied. "You didn't withdraw or play it cool. You let them know that they were affecting you. You became part of the picture instead of an outsider watching it all."

"It felt so good," Tom said.

"Both you and Duke have a tendency to withdraw. I'm so happy to see you both right in the middle of the action."

"I'm a lot older than you," said June, "and I still can't really talk to my parents. Since taking the class, I can talk to pretty much everybody else, even my husband. But I still close up when I deal with my parents."

"Parents are very often the hardest people for us to talk to," I said. "However, today we're beginning a whole new phase of the work which may help you get over that final hurdle. The reports that Duke and Tom have given make it particularly appropriate that we start on this new phase today."

"What is it?" asked Storm.

"Up till now, we've been working basically within ourselves. Duke and Tom have talked today about using their newfound freedom to connect more effectively and fully with the people they are close to. From now on, we'll continue to breathe and sound, but we'll use the breathing and sounding to connect with each other. Instead of just letting something happen within us individually, we will begin to let something happen between us, in pairings. In this way, we will bring the work much closer to everyday life."

"Uh oh," said Lisa.

"How do we do that?" asked June.

"You'll see soon enough. Stretch out on the floor now, and we'll begin the movement work. We'll get to the new phase after we finish sounding."

Communicating without Words

After the students had finished sounding, I told them to roll over and come to a sitting position, then choose a partner and sit knee to knee. Tom and June moved toward each other and sat cross-legged with their knees touching. Then Bill and Storm paired. Finally Duke and Lisa also sat with their knees touching.

"Now close your eyes and get back in touch with your breathing. Allow a sound to come out. When you feel centered in your breath and sound, slowly open your eyes."

Eyes opened slowly. Sounds faded quickly as people were confronted by the face of another person less than a foot away.

"Keep your sound going. If you lose it, close your eyes till you get it again, then open your eyes slowly."

Tom and June began to laugh. June tried to stop herself.

"It's okay. Let happen whatever wants to happen. It's just like the work you did lying down, except now two people are involved."

Bill and Storm looked very purposeful: both were trying hard. Storm was having trouble producing any sound. Duke had leaned back on his hands to put some distance between him and Lisa.

After a few minutes, people got a little more comfortable and were able to sound easily. But nothing much happened. I let the pairings go for about ten minutes, then told everybody to rest, and then we formed our circle.

"How did it feel?" I asked them.

"Weird," Tom replied.

"It's hard to keep making the sound when you're so close to somebody," said Bill.

"That's the whole point. Up to now, you've been able to do the work in your own private world. Now, you are going to take that freedom and bring it into a relationship."

"A relationship?" asked Bill.

"A communication. A sharing. How many people feel they know their partner better than they did before?"

"I feel like I know Storm better," said Bill. "But I'm not sure what it is I know about her . . . I guess I have a better sense of how she feels about things."

"I was starting to get angry at Duke," said Lisa. "The way he was sitting back. I really wanted to yell at him."

"Why didn't you yell?" I asked.

"It wouldn't have been polite."

"Politeness is the enemy of direct communication.
Politeness is what keeps us from really connecting. These pairings are a time when we
can connect directly from our guts to another's, without worrying about being polite."

"But what if there is no connection?" asked
Storm. "What if you sit there and sound and
nothing happens?"

"Something will happen. All you have to
do is allow it. It's the same as with the floor
work. As you build the energy between you
and the politeness drops away, something will
happen."

Fighting and Loving

The following week, things did begin to happen. Tom had paired with Storm, Bill with
June. Duke and Lisa were again partners. As
the couples began to trade breath and sound,
Tom and Storm began yelling at each other. It
started peacefully enough. Tom was laughing,
Storm was looking serious. Suddenly, Storm
started to scream and Tom started screaming
back. Bill and June, who were having trouble
getting into it anyway, turned to watch the
uproar. Duke and Lisa this time were making
soft, sweet sounds and looking lovingly into
each other's eyes. They kept their focus.

"Use your hands," I said to Storm and Tom.

Immediately, their hands came out, grabbed each other's, and the screaming was accompanied by a pushing match going back and forth. Duke and Lisa finally lost their concentration when Storm pushed Tom into them. The two of them pushed him away, then they went back to their loving contact.

Storm and Tom continued screaming at each other. Then Tom began to laugh. Storm screamed and Tom laughed until she began to laugh too. The fight was forgotten and they both rolled on the ground laughing.

Bill and June sat staring in amazement.

"What the hell is going on?" Bill asked. He looked over at Duke and Lisa, who were now hugging each other gently. "What kind of class is this, anyway?"

When we formed our closing circle, I began to explain:

"Since we don't use words, these scenes reveal the basic ways that people connect. *Basically, all the scenes are either love scenes or fight scenes,* since love and hate, or tenderness and aggression, are our primary ways of relating to each other."

"Were we fighting?" Tom asked.

"You were until you started playing, which is a form of loving."

"They seemed very young," said June. "It reminded me of my daughter when she was much younger."

"Again, without words, these scenes allow

us to regress to a more direct and powerful way of relating. The playing reminds people of children or sometimes of animals."

"But at first we weren't playing," said Storm. "I was really getting angry at you."

"Why?" asked Tom.

"You just kept laughing. I wanted to make you take me seriously."

"You seemed too serious," responded Tom. "I just wanted you to have a good time."

"That's why you had such an effective pairing," I pointed out. *"You each had an objective, something you wanted from the other person, and your objectives were in conflict.* That's what produces a fight scene."

"I don't understand what happened at the end of ours," said Tom. "We were fighting, then we were laughing."

"Well, I got tired of fighting," said Storm, "and you started laughing again, and I couldn't resist any longer. I started laughing too."

"Then I won," said Tom.

These scenes take on a life of their own. They tend to have a beginning, a middle, and an end—a conflict and a resolution. When the scene shifts, that's a signal that it is over and a new one is starting. The ending was indeed what Tom had wanted, but he had to go through a process to get there.

"How do you feel?" I asked Lisa.

"I feel embarrassed," she said, blushing. "I'm not used to getting so close to someone."

"Did you feel close to Duke?" I asked.

"Yes. And before the scene, I didn't even realize that I liked him." Her face reddened even more.

"It was amazing, really tuning into you," said Duke. "I always thought you were a little stuck-up."

"I'm really shy," Lisa said. "Sometimes people think I'm stuck-up."

"You didn't seem that shy today," I said.

"I surprised myself," said Lisa. "But I guess I'm not as shy as I used to be. Not since taking the class."

"I felt embarrassed by their pairing," Bill said. "It seemed very sexual to me."

"All pairings are sexual," I replied, "in the sense that intimacy is a breaking down of barriers. In our society, we have made it very hard to get close to someone else, except sexually. These exercises allow you to explore a close connection without having to get sexual."

"It still makes me nervous," Bill replied.

"I think we both found it really hard," said June. "It's hard to look into someone's eyes like that, let alone make sound."

"It is hard," I responded. "Our society puts up barriers to really seeing and being with another person. I have had students say they felt closer to their partner in the pairings than they did to their spouses."

"How can that be?" asked June.

"There is a lot of fear that surrounds most

relationships. Fear of fully being who you are. We're used to seeing our lovers and friends in limited ways. And we tend to avoid open conflict. As a result, it's difficult to get to know and love another person fully, shortcomings and all."

"And some of us have plenty of shortcomings," added Tom.

"Whenever my girlfriend and I begin to feel some distance from each other, we always do a pairing," I said. "It helps us really see each other as we are. She tells me that doing a pairing, she can always see how much I love her in my eyes, and it convinces her more than my saying it a thousand times."

"But what if she saw 'I hate you' in your eyes?" asked Storm.

"It could happen. At least at some point during the pairing. That's why couples are sometimes afraid of this exercise. You're not sure what is going to come out. The irony is that you cannot love someone without sometimes being very angry at them. *Love and hate are opposite sides of the same thing: closeness.* The anger that inevitably comes up when your wishes are thwarted has to be acknowledged and integrated into any successful relationship.

"My girlfriend and I used to try to get to the end of a fight without actually going through it, to 'make up' by sweeping our differences under the rug. But we found that by airing the differences and going through the fight, we felt a lot closer. Somebody once said that we have lovers' quarrels because the making up is so good, and there's a lot of truth to that.

"The books that opened my eyes to the importance of fighting are *Creative Aggression* and *The Intimate Enemy,* both by George Bach. He states beautifully how essential it is to fight and clear the air. He also suggests that all lovers' fights are basically distance fights, where one partner wants the other either to move back and give him or her more room or to move closer and make more of a commitment. When Duke's girlfriend told him she had slept with someone else, she was getting him either to move farther away or move closer."

"She sure got me a lot closer," Duke responded with a smile. "I guess I had been sitting on the fence in terms of committing to her. This pushed me over to her side."

"For myself," I continued, "I had always tried to be a 'nice guy' and my previous relationships had always collapsed under the weight of accumulated, unspoken resentments and grievances. This relationship I'm in now keeps getting better and better."

"I've always fought a lot in my relationships," said Storm. "And they didn't seem to get better. Eventually, we'd both get tired of the fighting and we'd break up."

"There is a difference between constructive or fruitful fights, which reach a resolution, and fruitless fights, which just go on and on."

"Those fruitless fights are the kind my parents have," Tom said.

"Many people are too scared to get beyond the fighting to the loving underneath," I responded. "They are afraid to surrender and show their vulnerability. The fighting serves as a love substitute. Even though it does not offer the deep closeness we would like, perpetual fighting provides steady contact with another person.

"My therapist used to tell how, as children, he and his best friend would walk home from public school and get into a fight every day. Each would come home bloody, and their worried parents tried to keep them apart. But they were living through the uncertainty and fear of the Depression, and they had a lot of anger and frustration to get out. And they could only get it out with each other. He said that he and his pal have stayed friends to this day."

"Do they still punch each other?" asked Tom.

"I hope not," I responded. "As I said last week, I am not an advocate of violence. What I'm getting at is that we need to make contact. Angry feelings always arise when people are close; we need to acknowledge and allow our anger. Otherwise, when we shut out our anger, we also shut out the person we want to be close to."

"But how do you get past the fighting? That's

what I want to know," said Storm.

"You just had the experience of going past the fighting."

"In the pairing?"

"Yes. What did you do there?"

"I fought and fought until it struck me as silly."

"You fought as long as you needed to and then your body moved on to the next thing. You can feel comfortable expressing your anger, but it is hard for you to let go of your anger and move on to another emotion. You did it in the pairing, though."

"I guess I did."

"You've seen kids play where they're best friends one minute and the next they're screaming 'I hate you, I don't ever want to talk to you again.' Then ten minutes later they're best friends again and all is forgotten."

"I've seen my daughter do that," Storm responded.

"They let each feeling flow through them and out."

"I guess I'm afraid to let go of my anger," said Storm, "because I'm afraid of what's underneath."

"What do you think that is?"

"A lot of need. A lot of vulnerability. A lot of hurt and longing for attention. I just don't want to give a lover the satisfaction of seeing me so needy."

"It's amazing you can see all that," said June.

"Yes, it is," I seconded. "It may indicate that you'll be more willing to surrender in the future."

Aggression and Surrender

In the following class, Bill, who kept a physical distance from the rest of the class, was paired with Duke. They were sitting knee to knee and making sound. Bill was obviously uncomfortable and Duke began to provoke him, using his face and voice to snarl and growl. At first, Bill laughed self-consciously, then he began growling back. The two men growled at each other, sounding like two bears defending territory. I suggested they use their hands. Immediately, Duke and Bill started to push each other, growling all the while.

Meanwhile, June found herself comforting Lisa, who had started to cry. The scene, with June gently rocking Lisa, looked like a perfect mother-daughter encounter.

Tom and Storm began to fight again. This time both of them went at it in earnest, pushing and shoving each other. After they had pushed for a while, tears began to trickle gently down Storm's cheeks. She stopped trying to fight Tom and just sat there crying. Tom embraced her and she held him also. The two of them rocked back and forth in an embrace.

Duke and Bill, however, got more seriously into their fight. Both stopped sounding. They rolled around on the ground. "Sound!" I kept yelling. "Sound!"

Finally Duke pinned Bill's arms, but Bill wouldn't give up. He kept straining to get up.

"Sound," I said. They began to growl again.

"Use words," I told them. "Use a phrase."

"Listen to me," Duke shouted. "Listen to me!"

Bill relaxed for the first time and let himself be pinned. "Okay, what do you want to say?"

Afterward, Bill asked me why I had told them to use words.

"I was getting a little nervous," I said. "And I knew that words would tone down the conflict. The scenes always get less physical when words are used. In fact, when students go in and out of words, I can watch the scene getting more civilized, then becoming more primitive again."

"I was becoming frightened that Duke would hurt me," Bill said.

"I was more afraid that you would hurt you," I said.

"What do you mean?"

"He had you pinned, but you just wouldn't surrender. You kept pushing against him. You had to give up or try something else. I was afraid you'd strain something."

"Does that happen often?" June asked. "Do people get pinned?"

"Yes, it does. If there's a fight that gets

physical and one person is stronger. Usually, when the person underneath lies still, the other will get up because it isn't much fun anymore. In the pairings, because they are less strong, many women find themselves having to yield more."

"That seems pretty dumb," said June. "Just brute strength."

"Part of fighting is knowing how and when to surrender. It's only brute strength if you let it be. You can change the action. Try a trick. Sometimes people lie still, pretend it's over, then jump the other person. But you do have to learn to surrender."

"It was hard to keep sounding," said Duke. "I kept losing it."

"I know. That's why I kept trying to remind you. *Without the sounding, you lose emotional awareness and spontaneity.* It becomes mostly a wrestling match. As you continue doing these pairings, it will become easier to sound even when you're fighting."

"What happened for you?" Lisa asked Storm.

"Well, Tom and I started out fighting again. We went at it for a while. Then I started to cry. I wasn't mad at him any more. I just felt little and sad."

"When I saw your tears, I felt very close to you," Tom responded. "I really wanted to comfort you."

"We started embracing," Storm finished. "It

was really nice."

I was moved by the encounter between Tom and Storm as well as by Storm's tender description of it. "Once Tom saw your vulnerability," I said to her, "he started to comfort you and the fight ended. You moved right past your anger, and the fight had a resolution."

"I guess it did," Storm agreed.

The mood of a pairing can shift suddenly. Just as emotions follow each other, so your relationships can change quickly from fighting to loving. Sometimes, it goes the other way. When people feel too close, they start to fight to create distance. The important thing is keeping the connection. Once aggressive feelings are expressed, it's easier for loving feelings to come into play.

EXERCISES

We reach out to others with our voices, our arms, our lips, and our pelvises. I developed the following exercise to give you a sense of what it is like to reach out. It comes from a blending of Reichian and Feldenkraisian principles.

Reaching Out

Lie down on the floor on your back.

Let your right arm come off the ground as if you were going to reach toward the ceiling, but don't reach yet. Let your shoulder blade touch the ground.

Reach up toward the ceiling and feel your shoulder blade pulling away from the ground. Don't strain. Immediately let your arm come back down so that the shoulder blade touches the ground. Your elbow is a little bent but basically straight. Reach again. Do this motion about five times or until your arm begins to tire. CAUTION: The arm tires very easily doing this. Pay attention to the signal. Don't overdo it. As soon as you feel tired, let your arm float to the ground and take a rest.

With the same arm, experiment with different ways of reaching. Rotate your arm as you reach up. Try rotating the hand clockwise as you reach, counterclockwise as you let go. Then reverse this. Experiment to find the easiest way to reach up.

Again, reach straight up and see if it has gotten easier.

Repeat the same two steps with the left arm. Rest as needed.

Now let your head roll to the left as you reach with the left arm. Then let your head roll right and see which makes the movement easier.

Reach with both arms simultaneously and see what that feels like. Let your head rock back and see if that makes the movement easier.

Now reach with your arms alternately, left and then right. Allow your head to roll.

Bend your knees and continue reaching. See how this changes the movement.

Now begin to reach in earnest, really sensing something which is just out of reach. Let the movement become larger and flowing. Feel yourself reaching out. Feel if there are other ways your body can reach. Reach out with your lips. Let your whole body reach. Find a sound which expresses the reaching your body is doing, and let that sound come out.

Pairings

This is the basic exercise I have developed to help you connect with another person. I have described earlier how this exercise can work. This exercise requires a partner, preferably someone you are close to, with whom you have been sharing—or at least talking about—this book.

Sit cross-legged on the floor, with your knees touching your partner's and your eyes closed.

Sense your skeleton in this position. Notice how the position of your pelvis has changed from when you lie on the floor. Sense the vertebrae stacked on top of each other and feel your head floating on top.

See your body as open and spacious and see your breath going in and out easily, without effort.

See your pool of vibrations deep down inside

you. Let the breath touch the vibrations, and let the sound touch you.

When you feel well connected with your breath and your sound, let your eyes open slowly. Look into the eyes of the other person while continuing your sound. If you find yourself becoming self-conscious and your sound disappearing, close your eyes. Reach out with sound to the other person, with your eyes still closed. Open your eyes when you feel ready. You can close and open your eyes several times until the connection is made.

Allow whatever wants to happen to happen. You don't have to plan. You may find yourself giggling nervously and that's fine. Whatever wants to happen. If you can, avoid simply mirroring the other person. Allow yourself to react to him or her.

You might have a sense of wanting something from the other person, and this will help you connect.

Allow the connection to grow. Don't worry if not a lot happens the first time. Once the barriers of self-consciousness and politeness begin to soften, you will find yourselves laughing together, screaming at each other, touching each other gently, or fighting. If you do feel like fighting, make absolutely certain you do not hurt yourself or the other person. Push rather than hit. Sit or kneel; do not rise to your feet. And make sure you are in a place where you have room to roll around safely. Keep breathing and keep sounding.

At some point, you may sense the pairing is over—when you've had enough. You can also have a third person begin the encounter and call a halt, or you can set a timer.

After you have done this exercise several times, you can begin to use words. Use them sparingly, however. It's most effective to use only a single phrase, repeated over and over.

When the exercise is over, you will find that you know your partner in a whole new way.

Taking It Further

Become aware of when you reach out to people and when you don't. Examine the feelings in your body when you reach out. Discover what you do with your breathing and your muscles to keep yourself from reaching out. You will find, as Duke and Tom did, that if you keep breathing, it is much harder to withdraw.

If fighting comes hard for you, let yourself fight. See the fight as an opportunity to get to know the other person better. Set up rules, including no physical violence and no knife-edged verbal attacks (for example, "I never liked sex with you anyway"). If fighting and anger are easy for you, see if you can get in touch with and express the feelings buried under the anger. In either case, read one of the books by George Bach mentioned earlier in the chapter.

An important way to reach out is to hug. We tend to be shy of hugs, except in sexual situations and with children. I will never forget when I was about nine years old and my father decided I was too old to be hugged. Instead, he bought boxing gloves so that we could spar. At the time, I thought he was right—after all, I was a "man" now. But the scars still linger.

Keep hugging your children, even when they get older. Hug your spouse as often as possible. Hug your friends. Use any excuse. Earlier, I spoke of the "touch hunger" which afflicts most of us. Hugging is a wonderful way to fill that hunger. There is a theory that we need four hugs a day just for survival, eight for maintenance, and twelve for growth. How many have you had today?

And when you do hug, really *hug*, without patting each other on the back or keeping your bodies carefully apart. *Hug, let your bodies touch, and breathe together.* A good hug can last for four or five deep exhalations or even longer.

You can reach out verbally by asking for what you want. Many of us expect others, especially spouses and friends, to read our minds. It is a lot easier to get what you want if you ask for it. If the answer is "no," don't be discouraged. You've found out where you stand instead of having to guess. And you can always ask someone else.

As you let yourself reach out more to other people, you will find that they respond. You will indeed be able to get the friendship and love you desire far more easily than you ever thought possible.

RESULTS

Lisa came into class radiant. When we commented on how alive she looked, she announced that she has just had a "great" fight with her boyfriend.

"I've been getting a lot angrier with him lately," she continued. "In the old days, I was very quiet and sulked for weeks. But now I just let him have it."

"Good for you!" cheered Storm enthusiastically.

"How is he taking it?" asked June.

"He got pretty upset at first. I was scared he was going to go away and never come back. But, after he got over the initial shock, he's been dealing with it pretty well. He can see that it ties up with my not having back pain anymore because I don't hold everything inside. And he likes it that I don't sulk so much.

"Also," she continued with a grin, "our sex life has been getting a lot better lately. He's pretty happy about that."

"Sex and anger do go together, don't they," said Storm thoughtfully.

"They're both created in the pelvis," I added.

"I've been having a very different kind of experience with my husband," June began. "He's

been getting much more gentle and affectionate. The other night he spent half an hour just
stroking me gently. It was really beautiful."

I was deeply touched by both stories. I was
struck by how much more love my students
seemed able to share. First Duke and Tom had
reported major changes. Now June and Lisa.
I felt both joyful and lonely—graduation was
not far away.

9

TRANSFORMING FEAR INTO CONFIDENCE

We often try so hard to make a good impression that we hold back the best parts of ourselves. This happens on dates, on job interviews, in public speaking, athletics, with friends—dozens of times a day, in fact. Ironically, the more we worry about how well we're doing, the worse we do. The more we are concerned with other people's opinions, the less we can truly communicate.

You can only rise to excellence when you stop "performing." Learning to be yourself confidently in any situation is the eighth step to personal power.

Embracing Yourself

June began class with a revelation. She had come in looking very determined and she spoke up immediately. "There's something I need to say," she began. "This is very hard for me to talk about, but I never really have talked about it with anyone, so I guess it's time.

"For many years, I have had a drinking problem. Almost nobody knows about it but my family and a few friends. It's not all the time. It's only some of the time. But if I'm upset or nervous, or if I'm in a social situation, I tend to drink too much.

"Well, I don't seem to have the problem anymore. I didn't really decide to stop or anything, it's just that I don't seem to want to drink so much anymore. I noticed it especially because of the Christmas holidays a while back. Usually, that's the worst time for me. But this year wasn't any problem. It just wasn't any problem."

There was a silence. We were all moved.

"That's great," I said, not knowing how to express my full enthusiasm.

"It's hard for me to even talk about it," June said. "Even to say that it's over. It's always been a hidden part of my life. I guess I would drink when I wanted to cry or get angry. And I would pretend it was the liquor, not me. That was the only time I used to fight, and my husband would think I got into the fights because of the liquor. Actually, I drank in order to have the courage to fight.

"But since I've been taking the class, I don't need liquor to be a bitch."

There was some laughter from the group,

which June joined in.

"I mean, I can accept how I feel. I can express my emotions and say, 'that's me.' I know I don't express that much here in class and sometimes I feel funny about that, but I really wanted you to know how much I've changed." Tears began to well up in her eyes. "And I guess the drinking was the final hurdle."

June hid her face in her hands. Spontaneously, the class burst into applause.

"I really am proud," said June, "and I want to thank all of you. The strange thing is, I'm proud, but I don't feel that I worked hard and somehow triumphed. It just happened."

"It didn't 'just happen' and you have plenty of reason to be proud," I responded. "What happened is that you became more comfortable with who you are and more willing to show it. You stopped needing the excuse of alcohol."

"I guess I did use alcohol as an excuse."

"Lots of people do. It's no accident that it was soon after Tom stopped overindulging in pot that he was able to confront his parents. The pot deadened his need to express his feelings. It allowed him to keep his 'cool' self-image intact."

"No more," Tom added.

Most of us get stuck in feeling that only one mode of behavior or one part of our being is acceptable. But we are wonderful, complex creatures, and all aspects of us demand expression. We can use drugs and alcohol to deaden a part of us or to allow it expression without being "responsible." But as we accept ourselves fully, we no longer need them.

"We all wear masks," I told the group, "which express only the part of us we think is most acceptable. The funny part is that when the mask drops away, the face underneath is not that much different.

"You really are a nice, thoughtful person," I said to June, "even if you are sometimes bitchy and nasty."

"Damn," said June, in mock frustration.

"And you really are 'cool,' Tom. You really are playful and funny, even if you do have a seriousness and vulnerability you have trouble admitting to."

"Shucks," Tom replied.

"I have pictures of myself growing up," I told the class, "and it's always fascinating to look at them. I can see how expressive I was as a young child. In the early pictures, I am beaming, happy to get so much attention. Later pictures with my baby sister and my family show me sad, alone, and burdened with responsibility. The pictures are so clear that it's amazing no one noticed. I looked troubled, shy, and out of place. And that's just how I felt. I was being myself, not putting on an act.

"Then, at around age ten or eleven, you can see me start to get fat and watch my face distort into a perpetual smile. The huge, toothy grin is my trademark for the next twenty years.

Every picture shows it. I had put on my mask and I kept it on. Now I look more like I used to at five than at any time in between.

"At ten or eleven years of age, I began to go through puberty. I could not let the world (or myself) realize that I was feeling sexual, that I was also very angry. There was too much of me that I couldn't accept. So I got fat and smiled a lot. There are a lot of people who make the same unconscious choice.

"Most of us have developed a self-image based on only some of our actions, emotions, and character traits. Parts of ourselves which do not fit into our self-image are either denied outright ('I never get angry') or serve as an occasion for guilt and self-criticism ('If I were a better person, I wouldn't get angry'). Our tightened muscles reflect our self-image. Our bodies become cages, keeping us from expressing our 'negative' qualities. Our faces become masks, only showing the world the part of us we want it to see."

"How does that happen?" asked June. "Why do we get so tightened up?"

"It happens over time," I replied. "As we try to fulfill expectations of other people. Our parents have a lot to do with it. As does the school system. Being quiet and sitting in one place is not something that children are designed to do.

"The whole point of my work is to undo the damage. To get us back to the place where

we are willing and able to express all of ourselves. Over time, our bodies have tightened
so that we can no longer say what we mean or
ask for what we want. I am not teaching you
to run amok, but to be able to make a choice."

"I know that my self-image involves being
special," said Duke. "I think that's why I have
so much trouble writing. I write in order to be
special, and if I can't write, then I feel I'm just
ordinary. Somehow, in my upbringing, being
ordinary was the greatest sin of all. Well, lately
I've begun to feel that I really am ordinary.
And there's some comfort in it. If I'm ordinary,
I don't have to try so hard."

"You are ordinary," I responded. "You eat
and you eliminate, just like everyone else."

"That's funny," June said.

"About eating and eliminating?" Tom asked.

"No, it's that I always thought I was so ordinary. I always thought I was an ordinary girl.
Then an ordinary wife and mother. It's only
since taking the class that I've begun to realize
how special I am, how many talents I have."

"We are all ordinary," I said. "We all have
basically the same needs and desires. We all
need to be loved and respected. We all need
to make a difference. We all want to be happy
and lead a fulfilling life.

"But we all go after our goals differently.
And our definitions of love and happiness are
all a little different. In those respects, we are
all of us very special. And often the parts of

us we don't like are integral parts of that specialness.

"Weaknesses and strengths are often the same traits. What seems to be bitchiness in one situation could be seen as standing up for yourself in another. We need to have a wide range of traits in order to have a wide range of ways to respond to different situations."

"I've really started to accept and enjoy those times when I start arguments," June said.

"We need a self-image that loves all of us, as we are," I responded. Then I told the class the story of my work with Anna, who was one of my most interesting students. Anna was an anorexic, whom I worked with privately. Anorexia is the most extreme eating disorder. The victim cannot accept herself as needing food at all. Anorexics often get very sick, and may actually starve themselves to death.

Anna, like many anorexics, wanted to be a boy. When I gently pointed out to her that this was impossible, she broke into long, sustained weeping, which was the first full emotion she was able to express.

Anna felt that not eating made her special. It was as if she didn't need what other people did. Also, because of lack of food, she did think differently from other people. She was often semi-incoherent.

As Anna got more in touch with her body, she first felt the pain in her stomach. After crying hopelessly for a few weeks, she began to get angry and scream and hit the pillows. At that point, she realized how little damage she could do. She began to experience how weak she was. She began to have dreams of being pushed around and not being able to push back. And she realized how much she was pushed around by her friends.

"I know how you can get stronger," I told her.

"Eat more," she replied.

And she began to eat again. The physical realization of weakness had cracked the self-image and gotten through to her. It was a pleasure to see her fill out week by week. While she remained thin, she lost that "refugee" look. She is now a quite successful fashion model.

When I finished the story, several of my students laughed.

"It's true," I continued. "Society sets up the image which helps lead girls into anorexia. But she had gotten past the pathological state. She could accept her kinship with all living things— she had to eat."

When you try to live up to a self-image, it is like you are split into two parts: the actor and the critic. The actor is always trying to gain the critic's approval.

June was worrying so much about what other people might think of her, that she was unable to be herself without drinking. As she was able to tune into herself more, she was able to cut way down on her drinking.

Anna was an extreme example of someone living (actually, almost dying) to please an internal critic.

As both June and Anna learned to breathe, sound and gain more body awareness, they began to lose the feeling that they were always being watched and evaluated. And they stopped constantly watching and evaluating themselves.

Communicating Instead of "Performing"

The next step for my students was to be able to keep the sense of comfort, privacy, and self-esteem they had gained, even when they were actually performing—to go beyond stagefright, no matter what the situation.

The following week, Lisa came into class looking both excited and nervous. She announced that she was up for a promotion.

There was general excitement in the class.

"It's a position in marketing research," she explained. "It's a lot more creative than what I'm doing now. And it pays a lot better. Anyway, my boss has noticed all the changes I've made in the last few months. And he thinks I might be ready for it."

"Terrific," said Duke.

"But it's not really up to him," Lisa said. "He's just suggesting me. I've got to talk, to interview for it. And with his boss's boss. One of the vice-presidents of the company. I'm terrified. I'm really terrified."

Lisa was indeed scared. Her whole body was quivering.

"I don't know if I can do it," she said.

"Of course you can," said Tom. "I mean, that's what you've been working on for the past six months."

"But I'm so nervous. I'm afraid I won't be able to say anything. I'll just sit there."

"It's okay to be nervous," I said.

"But it's not okay to sit there and not say anything," Lisa replied.

"Look, what's the worst that can happen?" asked Duke.

"I'll wet my pants," Lisa replied.

"You really won't be as scared as that," I replied. "You've changed a lot since you first came to class."

"Yeah," said Tom. "For a while I wasn't even sure that you could talk."

Lisa chuckled ruefully. "Very funny," she said.

"Now you're really expressing yourself," Duke said. "Some of those pairings have been really amazing."

"I feel safe in here," Lisa said. "Well, as safe as I ever feel. And I've noticed that it's easier for me to talk to people most of the time. But this is the vice-president. Even my boss is scared of him."

"He's just a person," Storm said.

"Easy for you to say," Lisa replied.

"You know, it's funny," Bill put in. "I'm going through a lot of nervousness also. I've got to give another presentation next week."

"I thought you told us that giving presentations had become a breeze since taking the class," said Tom.

"Well, it has. But up to now it was for only ten or twenty at the most. This time I've got myself into giving a lecture to three hundred people."

Tom whistled.

"That's a lot of people," Duke put in.

"I know that three hundred people seems overwhelming to most of us," Storm said. "But why should the number of people make that much difference?"

"I don't know, but it does," said Bill. "Maybe it's because I'm used to making personal contact. It's hard to make personal contact with three hundred people."

"Now I feel really stupid," Lisa said. "Bill is talking about speaking in front of all those people and I'm afraid to go on a stupid interview."

"The number of people isn't really important," I responded. "We all have some point at which we get performance anxiety.

"You see, we spend most of our lives 'performing,' doing things in front of other people. For some people, at certain times, the other people just fade away and they are just doing what they want. When you lie on the beach and close your eyes, you may lose all awareness that other people may be watching you. Most of us, however, are aware of other people and their responses most of the time.

"This class is always working on performance anxiety. Personally, I used to feel on display, like people were watching and judging me. When I started doing the physical awareness exercises, I would always look around the room to see how everyone else was doing. I was always comparing my performance with theirs. That's one of the reasons I have you close your eyes when you're doing the exercises. You can't see anybody, and your unconscious believes that nobody can see you.

"In the pairings, we actually confront each other with our eyes open. As you've learned from doing this, *the more you tune into your own signals, the less you worry about what other people are thinking of you, and the better you do.*

"The problem still comes up for me sometimes when I'm jogging and someone whizzes past me, or when I'm playing tennis and some hotshots take the next court. I begin to wonder what they're thinking of me, and my game deteriorates. Or I start to run too fast and end up out of breath."

"What's the difference what they think of you?" said Storm.

"Exactly. One, there is no reason their opinion should be important to me. Two, they're probably too busy doing what they're doing to even really notice. Yet I often still have to make a conscious effort to breathe deeply and get back into myself."

"I can understand all that," said Bill. "But Lisa and I are in a different situation. We're not dealing with people who just happen to be around. Lisa's job is on the line. And I'm going to have three hundred people just sitting there staring at me."

"Your situation does sound pretty ominous when you describe it like that," I said. "Let's see what I can show you that will help you both be brilliant."

It's Okay to Be Afraid

"First of all, most people are nervous in a performance situation. If you are nervous, your audience knows it immediately. They don't dislike you for it. In fact, it makes you more human. But if you try to hide it, the audience sees you pretending not to be nervous when they know you are. You know that they know you're nervous, so the anxiety gets worse. It becomes a vicious circle. *The best thing to do with nervousness is to acknowledge it.*"

"You mean, tell the audience you're nervous?" Bill asked incredulously.

"You don't have to tell them. But you do need to acknowledge it to yourself and accept it as how you feel. *As soon as you acknowledge your anxiety, it will immediately begin to lessen.*"

"But what do you do with it?" asked Lisa.

"Just let it be. Let it run its course. Don't try to repress it or speak as if it's not there. My own technique is to sigh."

"You sigh in front of an audience?" asked Tom. "Don't they think you're weird?"

"Not really. They may see it as my little idiosyncrasy. If it doesn't seem appropriate, I take a soundless, deep exhale. Maybe several."

The implications of what I was saying suddenly struck June. "You mean *you* get nervous in front of an audience?" she asked in astonishment.

"Of course I do," I responded. "We've talked a lot about energy in here. Well, being in a performance situation is one of the biggest energy rushes there is. Speaking in front of an audience, going on a job interview, taking a test—all of these produce a fight or flight reaction in the body. Huge quantities of adrenaline and cortisone are pumped into the bloodstream. The whole body changes.

"The difference between a good performer and a bad performer is that the good performer loves the rush of energy. When he doesn't judge it as bad or try to fight it, his muscles stay relaxed and his breathing stays deep, and he is able to let the energy run deliciously through his body. It's a rush that is addictive for actors.

"The bad performer tries to fight the energy rush. His body is not free enough to let the energy move. And he tightens against it."

"Are you saying that anxiety is just energy flowing?" asked Storm.

"Anxiety is an interpretation of energy flow. We've talked about how all emotions are manifestations of energy flow. Well, with anxiety, the connection is the clearest. The nervous sensations of anxiety can be smoothed into the pleasurable tingles of energy moving. Fritz Perls, the founder of Gestalt psychology, put it into a beautiful formula:

Anxiety + Oxygen = Excitement"
"Amazing," said Tom.

"I remember going on stage several times when I wasn't nervous," I continued. "I was terrible. There was no energy, no 'oomph.' "

The color began to come back to Lisa's face. "So being nervous can be a positive," she said, "if I just acknowledge it and let it flow through me."

"Exactly," I responded.

"Well, it sounds a little weird," said Bill, "but I guess I can do it."

"I don't know," Lisa said, tensing up again. "It's all very well to say. But if I really let the energy go through me, I might pass out. What if I just sit there and can't say anything?"

"You can do it," I responded. "That's what the months of training have been for. Your body knows now how to let energy flow through it. All you have to do is to keep breathing. If you find yourself getting overwhelmed by the nervousness, *stop and breathe.*"

"You mean, just stop talking," said Bill.

"Absolutely. You can wait for the end of a sentence. But stop and breathe. The tendency when you get nervous is to keep talking and actually speed up. You hope to get to the end before your nervousness shows. But that's like speeding up when your brakes are gone on your car and you want to get home before you have an accident.

"You need to stop, breathe, and refocus on yourself and what you are trying to say."

Storm brought her eyebrows together, as she always did when something troubled her. "I still don't feel comfortable about revealing nervousness. I speak with customers, with employees, and with suppliers. And I am nervous sometimes. And I'm always afraid that no one would listen to me if they realized how nervous I was."

"You know, Storm," I replied, "even though your voice deepens by the end of each class, you still meet the world with a little girl voice. It's a voice which reveals none of your power. If you revealed more nervousness, you might also reveal more power."

"I see what you're saying," said Storm. "Sometimes I feel like all I'm doing is acting. Even though I'm a really good boss, I'm afraid people are going to find out I'm just a little girl pretending to be a boss."

Revealing Yourself

Many of us have the same fear as Storm. We're afraid people are going to discover how little and scared and incompetent we really are. So we hide who we are and present a mask to the world.

I've worked with a lot of actors. I always tell them that there are hundreds of actors auditioning for each part. If they're going to be cast, it's because there is something unique about them, which only they can reveal. Once they try to "act"—to be something they're not—they are at best an imitation of someone else.

For any speaking or performing, the most important first step is to give up your image of being a "good speaker" or "good actor" or "good singer." I remember when I started singing lessons. Fortunately, my singing teacher had a tape recorder and I was able to listen to how I sounded. Every time I thought I was "really singing"—really belting it out and singing like I thought a singer would—it sounded terrible. Every time I felt I wasn't doing enough—just communicating the meaning, not "singing" at all—it sounded wonderful on the playback.

I explained all this to Lisa, but she remained unsure. "What do I do? What do I say?" she kept asking.

"Do you want the job?" I asked.

"Oh, yes," Lisa said with enthusiasm.

"Then say that. Do you think you can handle it?"

"Yes, I do," said Lisa, surprised at her own conviction. "I've got a lot of ideas about marketing research."

"Then say that too. All you have to do is reveal to the boss your enthusiasm and your belief in yourself. I believe that performance is about revealing yourself. We tend to keep ourselves hidden. I've seen several well-known actors who were extremely boring in person. What happens? It is my belief that it is only in playing a role that they have permission to reveal themselves. The interesting, exciting parts of them are hidden in everyday life. That is one of the reasons actors act. So they can be who they really are."

"I really do know a lot about marketing research," said Lisa. "I had two classes in school, and I've studied a lot on my own. But I don't want to sound uppity."

For many people, the hardest thing to reveal about ourselves is our accomplishments. In the first flyers for my class, I didn't mention that I held a doctorate. I was afraid it would be too imposing and scare people off.

I told the class this and also gave them an example of one of my private clients. He was an engineer who was preparing for an interview for a job promotion. I had to keep pushing and probing before he revealed that he had already been doing work at the level for which he was seeking the promotion. He was hiding the experience that clearly qualified him for the new position for fear of stepping on someone's toes or seeming to brag.

"I understand that one," said Duke, when I had finished. "I'll trot out my neuroses and inadequacies real quick, but I never talk about my accomplishments. I'm always afraid of blowing my own horn."

"When I was a kid," said June, "I always used to laugh and clown around. Then one day I remember a neighbor telling my mother that she should 'get the little show-off to shut up.'"

"I'm glad you shared that with us," I said. "Actors spend much of their lives playing 'look at me, Mommy.' And there's nothing wrong with that, so long as you don't get stuck in it. It's really very healthy for kids to be the center of attention. However, adults often get into the old 'children should be seen and not heard' syndrome. Many of us grow up terrified of attracting attention or being noticed. Paradoxically, as adults we need to be noticed in order to be successful. Our childhood training interferes with our adult living."

Winning Your Audience

"There's one more thing," said Lisa. "The man who's going to interview me is really intimidating. It's not just me. *Everyone* finds him intimidating."

"Just remember one thing," I responded. "He is a man with a problem."

"He is?" said Lisa, surprised.

"Of course. He has a job that he needs to fill. *He is not looking to eliminate people. He's looking to find someone who will do the job.*"

"I guess that's true," said Lisa.

"Of course it is," I replied. "You could be the solution to his problem."

"I never thought of it that way."

"The same thing applies to you, Bill," I said. "Your audience is not there to judge you. They want something. They want to learn something and to enjoy themselves doing it. *They are rooting for you to do a good job since that will be of most benefit to them.*"

"But what if I don't do a good job?" asked Bill. "I don't want to disappoint them."

Lisa still looked puzzled. "It's really hard for me to believe that this guy is really on my side."

"Okay," I replied. "There is another position you can take toward the audience. I have coached many actors through auditions where the casting director needed to control and dominate. Even though he or she needed the role cast, their ego needs kept them from being on the actor's side.

"For those situations, I developed what I call the 'Fuck You' school of acting."

There was general laughter.

"Sounds great," said Tom.

"It can be very effective," I replied. "Instead of worrying about the audience or getting caught up in trying to please them, you go in with the attitude of 'Fuck you, I know I'm great and you're lucky to have me here.' I've given a lot of successful performances starting with that attitude."

Everyone laughed again, including Lisa. She obviously liked that attitude.

"But isn't that a little hostile?" asked June.

"Yes," I replied. "But sometimes you need some hostility to break yourself of worrying too much about your audience. If realizing they are on your side doesn't do it—or if they really are not on your side—this attitude can help. Whichever attitude you choose, the important thing is to pay more attention to yourself and worry less about the opinions of others. *Paradoxically, the less you worry about others, the better you do with them.*"

Knowing What You Want

"But if you don't worry about others, what do you do?" asked June. "You've got to worry about something. I mean, you've got to keep your mind occupied."

"Focus instead on what you want. What is the purpose of your performance? What are you trying to accomplish? What do you want from your audience?

"In acting terms, this is called your 'objective.' Stanislavsky, who is the founder of modern actor training, says that the objective is the single most important tool the actor has. Staying focused on your objective is not only important for acting, but for everyday life. It's very hard to get what you want if you don't know what that is."

"What do I want?" asked Lisa. "I want to get the job."

"Good," I responded. "How are you going to make that happen?"

Lisa looked blank.

"What is your purpose during the interview?" I asked.

"To get it over with as quickly as possible," Lisa answered truthfully.

Tom and Duke laughed.

"That is not what I would call a useful objective. It's not the kind of purpose which will help you get the job. You see, your audience perceives your objective, even if you don't say it. If you just want to finish and get the hell out of there, that's what the interviewer will perceive."

"What's my purpose during this presentation?" asked Bill. "To show them how expert I am so that they'll think of me when they need work in my area," he answered himself.

"And how are you going to do that?" I asked.

"What do you mean?" he asked.

"In addition to knowing what you want," I replied, "it's very useful to have an image of how it's going to happen. For instance, when I teach you, I want to help you learn. But how am I going to do that? I can get you to see the light. I can share my enthusiasm with you. I can set you on a path. I can push you or pull you or guide you. Each of these is an image that helps make my objective more specific."

"Okay," said Bill. "I'm going to dazzle them with my brilliance."

"Great," I responded, enjoying his audacity. "Whenever you stop and breathe deeply, you can just flash on your purpose."

"Won't Bill have trouble with a purpose like that?" asked Duke. "Won't it make him self-conscious?"

"Not if he believes he can do it," I replied.

"I couldn't handle an objective like that," Lisa said.

"Then don't choose it. If you're not comfortable with an objective, it's not right for you. The purpose of an objective is to focus you quickly and pleasantly on why you are performing and to stop you from worrying. How do you want to go about getting your job?"

"I want to show him that I know my stuff, even though I'm shy." Lisa replied.

"So you want to reveal your inner strength," I suggested.

"Yeah," said Lisa. "And I want to show him that he needs me. I mean, I'm doing really well at my present job, and I really want this promotion."

"So you'll share your inner strength and enthusiasm with him."

Lisa smiled. "That sounds good," she said.

Breaking the Barriers

When it came time for the pairings, I assigned the students, rather than let them choose partners. I had Bill and Lisa, who had never paired before, work together. At first the two were very tentative. Then Lisa began to sneer at Bill and stick her tongue our provocatively. Bill began to growl back. Before long the sound had escalated, and their faces were almost touching.

I surreptitiously tapped the other couples on the shoulder and had them stop pairing and watch Bill and Lisa. The two continued for another minute. Then Bill became aware that something had changed. His eyes moved away from Lisa. Finally, he broke contact and looked at the audience looking back at him.

"What the hell?" he said. "What the hell is going on?"

"You've just reached the final stage of the work," I responded, "which is doing a pairing in front of the group. Now you not only go out to another person, but you do it with an audience watching. I felt that you two would be best suited to inaugurate this stage."

"You sneaky bastard," Bill said, shaking his head.

"You rat," Lisa chimed in.

"I'll take compliments later," I replied. "You guys aren't finished yet. Get back to it."

Sighing deeply, Bill and Lisa turned to face each other again.

"Close your eyes and get back in touch with the vibrations of your sound," I said. When they had, I told them to open their eyes again.

This time, the difference was amazing. Both were self-conscious and jittery. Lisa couldn't keep a sound coming out. Bill kept darting glances at the group out of the corner of his eyes.

After no more than a minute of awkwardness, however, the two began to make contact again. Now, fed by the energy of the audience and their own adrenalin rushes, Bill and Lisa expressed their aggression even more strongly. Lisa stuck out her tongue again. Bill began to shake her. They grappled, rolling around on the floor. The aggression soon broke and the two found themselves hugging each other tightly, moaning soft endearments to each other.

"Rest," I said.

They kept on hugging. Tom and Duke began to snicker.

I had to tell them to rest twice more before Lisa and Bill were ready to release each other and turn to the group.

"How do you feel?" I asked.

"Wonderful," Lisa answered, her eyes shining.

"Great," said Bill. "After a minute, I forgot all about the audience. I just got involved with Lisa. And it felt wonderful to get so close. It isn't easy for me."

"I forgot about the group also," said Lisa. "I didn't think it was possible, but I did. But, boy, was I angry with you."

"I don't blame you," I responded. "It was a dirty trick. But I wanted to show you how the audience can fade out. What we just worked on is what Stanislavsky called 'concentration.' Concentration on another person or on an objective (a goal or desire) is the best antidote to stagefright. I realize that in your professional presentations, you will both have to look right at your audience, so the situations will be different from what you did here. But I wanted to give you a sense of how effortless it can be to perform."

"I didn't feel like I was performing at all," said Lisa.

"Did you notice how intense your pairing got after you realized that the audience was watching you?"

"It sure did," Bill replied.

"Well, you both had the benefit of being the focus of the audience's energy as well as having adrenalin rushes of your own. Your energy levels increased, so more could happen between you. You both had the experience of how *presenting to an audience can actually enable you to be more of who you are.*

"One of the reasons I teach is that I love what my students bring out in me. Rather than an obstacle, an audience can be a 'facilitator,' allowing you to bring out the best in yourself."

EXERCISES

Since you will probably be performing with words, not just sounds, here is the exercise I use to help my students keep the power and truthfulness they attain in the sounding when they are working on scripted material.

Performance

Take a story or song that you like and recite it to an imaginary audience and/or to a supportive, patient friend. Consider three things: 1) what the story or song is about; 2) why you like it; and 3) what you want to convey to your audience.

Begin by getting in touch with your breathing and allowing a sound to come out. Then open your eyes and sound at the audience—real or imaginary. If the audience is real, you may feel like laughing for a while.

When you feel centered, continue to sound, and as you are exhaling, speak the first line of text. If you are reading from a book, memorize as much of the first line as you can do easily, then put the book down, look your audience in the eye, begin to sound and speak the line right to them.

Repeat this technique throughout the piece.

This performance exercise may seem a little strange at first, but it will allow you to speak with feeling, without worrying about how you "should" be saying the lines.

You can use the same technique for improvised material. Start with sounds and let the sound become words.

Taking It Further

In a sense, we are performing all the time since we spend much of our lives connecting with other people. Ironically, the less you try to put on a performance, the better you do. I have given you many practical suggestions for performance situations in the previous section of this chapter, and I invite you to practice them at every opportunity. Let me sum them up:

Anxiety + Oxygen = Excitement

Everyone gets nervous when performing. A good performer knows how to use his nervous energy, not fight it.

Performing involves not hiding but revealing yourself.

Your audience wants something from you.

They are not in the position of power—you are.

Instead of worrying about your audience, focus on what you want from them.

RESULTS

"Well, I did it," Lisa said, when we met the following week. "I made it through the interview."

"How did it go?" Storm asked.

Lisa's face broke into a broad grin. "It was great. I was nervous, but I didn't let it bother me. I was able to tell him that I wanted the job and that I thought I would be good for it. I even figured out an objective. I showed him I was the solution to his problem. I don't know about the job yet, but I could tell he was impressed. I feel wonderful. It gives me a whole new sense of myself. When I saw that I impressed him, I began to think that maybe I was impressive."

"Wonderful," I said. "When we're children we get a good deal of our sense of self-worth from others. They respond to our behavior. Then we internalize their opinions. That's how we often get stuck. It's great to get some really positive feedback. I'm glad that you already feel more impressive."

"You look more impressive," said Duke, only half joking. There was something more powerful and positive about Lisa.

"Thanks," Lisa said. "Actually, I think I'm still in shock. I didn't think I could do it."

"How did your presentation go, Bill?" asked June.

"It was fantastic," said Bill, still in awe at his own achievement. "I did it! I actually did it. I said everything I wanted to say. I was brilliant. And they loved me. I can't believe it."

"I've got something to report also," said Storm, "even though it's not quite as impressive as what Bill and Lisa reported. I've been thinking a lot about what we said last week. And I've been applying it to my tennis game. I've always worried about what other people were thinking. I'd give myself a running commentary, almost as if I were a trainer: Step forward; get your arm back sooner; you blew that one, dummy. Well, this week I've been concentrating on enjoying myself and letting my body do what feels good. And you know what? My game has improved a hundred percent. I'm amazed at some of the shots I get now that I've stopped trying so hard."

"I have something to report also," said Tom. "When I got into this class, I was interested in acting. I mean, I pretended it was just casual, like a hobby. But I really am interested. I've been taking some private acting training with Bret, and I think I'm getting pretty good.

"Anyway, I have a friend in the film business and he told me about a feature film which I might be right for. I called them and they wanted me to give them a picture and a resumé. Well, I don't have a resumé, since I haven't acted in anything except two high school plays. Also, I don't have a resumé picture. All I could find to give them was a snapshot my sister took of me in sunglasses." He took out the snapshot and showed it to the class.

"You're thinking of giving them that?" I asked.

"It's all I have, and I have to get something over there tomorrow morning. You think I shouldn't do it?" Tom asked, worry creeping into his voice.

"In all my years connected with theatre, I've never seen anyone turn in a picture like that," I responded. "But maybe I'm just being stuffy. Give it a try; there's nothing to lose."

"That's how I feel," said Tom. "After all, I'm just doing as you say. I'm just trying easy."

10

GETTING WHAT YOU WANT

In all of life, nothing gives me as much pleasure as helping people to change and grow. From the time I was a little child, I was always teaching others. And yet, for years I refused to recognize this part of myself. I always found myself teaching, yet that never seemed like a good enough occupation. Only through my personal experience of the techniques I teach did I come to accept my mission. After that, everything fell into place.

I remember how stuck I felt after my graduation from Yale. I watched my friends begin to gain success as writers, directors, and actors, while nothing seemed to happen for me. It got so bad that I couldn't even read the drama section of the *New York Times*. I couldn't stand to read about my fellow drama students while I lingered in obscurity.

It was only through my experiences with body awareness, movement, breathing, and sounding that I came to realize that I wasn't "making it" because I didn't really want to. I actually had other desires and interests. Writing, acting, and directing, for all their glamour, never gave me the kind of satisfaction I got from teaching.

I felt that the train had left without me, and I was destined to remain behind. But the train had been going in the wrong direction. Once I learned to follow my impulses, it didn't take me long to move quickly in the direction I wanted to go.

Recently, I was talking to someone who felt she was a failure. I asked her what that meant to her. As we talked, it became clear that she saw success as society defined it: money, prestige, power. I suggested that success might be doing what you love and being with people you love. Her face lit up. She felt that by those standards, she was pretty successful. When she saw herself as successful, she was. And some of the external trappings of success soon began to come her way.

Learning to listen to your inner voice and define your own success is the ninth step to personal power. If you have been following the exercises in this book, you have already begun to define your own success. You are now less dependent on other people's opinions and more willing to seek out what really makes you happy. Often, we cannot get what we want because we have no idea of what it is we want. Sometimes, we are doing exactly what we want, but we can't accept or realize it. We keep looking outside for success while success is already with us, if only we could see it. You are now in a position to know what you want and go for it.

You have begun to learn, on a physical level, that you have a choice. As you have freed your breathing, movement, emotions, and energy flow, so you have also freed yourself to reach out for what you need and ask for what you want. Like my students, you are now ready to graduate.

Lisa got the promotion. She came in the following week glowing. She was due to start the new job the next day.

"I feel a little scared," she said. "But I feel ready. I feel really different. Like the new job is just an extension of the new me."

Lisa did indeed appear different. Her presence showed new determination and confidence.

Lisa was not the only one with good news. Duke, who was most comfortable when he was deadpan, was grinning from ear to ear.

"I've got something to report also," he said. "I hadn't been able to write anything for months. I had just about given up on it. Well, last weekend I got the first story idea I've had in months. I sat down at the typewriter, wrote the first sentence, and it all disappeared. There was nothing. I felt cold and clammy, like I was in prison. So I started to check out my body and I realized that I wasn't breathing and my gut felt like steel.

"I realized that I was already worrying. I'd only written one line, but my mind was racing ahead. Would the story be a good one? What would the editor of *Harper's* think of it? Perhaps the style was too snappy. Perhaps it wasn't snappy enough.

"Rather than enjoying the process of writing, I was worrying about what other people would think. I remembered what you had said about performance, Bret. Writing had always been a misery for me; suddenly I understood why.

"Well, I started to breathe. I moaned and groaned. I let my shoulders and gut relax and focused on what I wanted to say. I saw that all the anxiety I was experiencing was potential excitement, and I breathed into it.

"Then I began typing again, staying with my enjoyment of the physical process of writing, the way it fills me and makes me warm. I wrote thirty pages over the weekend."

"That's wonderful," June smiled. "I wish I could write."

"Look at Bret," said Storm. "He's grinning just like you are, Duke."

I was indeed happy. Time after time, I have been stunned by the results of the techniques I teach. It is amazing to see such organic change. By helping someone free up physically, I also set in motion changes on a feeling level. These changes are followed inevitably by changes in behavior. Body, breathing, and voice become both more relaxed and more powerful. The student becomes more able to express emotions and experience pleasure. And the major changes in accomplishment come like icing on the cake.

I shared my thoughts with the class. I told them of how stuck I had felt after Yale, and how happy I was finally to be on the right train. My students had a lot of trouble accepting the idea that I had gone through the same process they were finishing.

"You felt stuck?" said June incredulously.

"Completely stuck," I responded. "And I thought it was too late. I thought I had missed my chance."

"I used to feel like that all the time," said Duke. "It's been changing, though."

"I still feel like that sometimes," said June. "Of course, I'm a lot older than you."

"Well, I felt stuck and left behind when I turned twenty-one," said Lisa. "So I guess it's not just a question of age."

"Yeah, I felt stuck too," Tom said. "Until I got this part."

There was a silence.

"You what!" I exclaimed.

"I got the part," Tom responded, letting his excitement show. "I blew the director away. He said he'd never seen anyone so easy and natural. He couldn't believe it. I had a callback the next day. Then he told me I had the part. We start shooting next month."

The class erupted with handshakes and hugs. Finally, things began to calm down.

The incredible joy I felt suddenly gave way to a sweet sadness. I could feel my emotion echoed in the room.

"You know," I said, "we've been together nine months now. That seems like a pretty significant length of time. I think it's time for graduation."

"Are you kicking us out?" asked Storm.

"Of course not," I answered. "You're welcome to continue, or to come back for refresher work any time you want. I only meant that you've all come to a closing. If you continue, you will be working at a new level."

There was a silence. I felt like a parent whose children have grown up.

"Let's have a party," said Tom. "A graduation party."

"Great," I responded. "Let's all bring something to eat next week."

"And diplomas," said Tom. "We've got to have diplomas."

"I'll see what I can do," I said.

"I don't feel like I'm ready to graduate," said Storm. "I don't feel I've come as far as some of the others. My voice still goes high most of the time. And I still have trouble with men."

"Is it okay with you?" I asked.

"What?" Storm replied.

"Is it okay with you that your voice goes high and you still have trouble with men?"

"Yes, I guess it is," Storm said, after thinking for a moment. "I can accept myself much more now. It doesn't bother me like it used to."

"If you can accept yourself and acknowledge the need to change without beating yourself up for your 'faults,' then you have done all you need to do in here. Everyone has their own rhythm of change. Everyone in the class will continue to change from the work we have done. Just as I continue to change. You have the tools. You just have to follow your own rhythm."

"Sometimes that's hard to do," said June. "Especially when you're older."

"You know me," said Storm. "I need to learn patience and I want it now. I hate it that everything takes so long. I feel like there just isn't enough time."

"I always used to feel that time was against me," I replied. "That's why I felt stuck. I felt that time was racing by, leaving me behind. I've come to understand that time is really on my side. Time only gets to be a problem when I keep looking toward the future instead of living in the present. I am good enough today, and I may be even better tomorrow."

"I feel that I've come a very long way since I started this class," said Lisa. "But now I'm starting to work at a whole different level. It's scary to think of giving up the class with all the new challenges and responsibilities in my life."

"You don't have to give it up, as I said. But even if you do, you have the tools you need to keep growing and coping with challenges."

"I'll be sorry to leave," said Lisa. "I've come to a lot of amazing changes through the class. Though it has been painful sometimes."

"Unfortunately, there has to be some pain in making all these changes," I said. "As we get older, we tend toward inertia. There is an element of change which is painful or at least disconcerting. I always look at the pains of changing as growing pains, just as muscles ache when you stretch them after long disuse."

"Well, it's been worth it," said Bill. "All of it." He had been unusually silent. I noticed there were tears in his eyes.

"You know," said Tom, "I've been getting this amazing feeling lately. You know how cynical I used to be. Well, lately, I've been getting this feeling that the whole universe makes sense, that there's a purpose and beauty to it all. I'd like to explain it to my friends, but I don't feel I can. I'm afraid they'd just laugh at me. But I have these incredible moments when everything seems to make sense, when everything seems good and beautiful."

"I know what you mean," said Duke. "I feel that way sometimes when I'm with my girlriend. Or when I'm hiking in the woods."

"You know what I mean?" said Tom, relieved.

"I think everybody here does," I said.

Lisa, June, and Bill nodded their heads in assent.

"When I was teaching at Tufts," I went on, "I had many moments of despair and confusion. Whenever I would think about what I was doing, it seemed ridiculous. Any accomplishments I made or could make seemed a mere speck in the cosmos, insignificant in the order of things. Now, when I stop doing and just ponder, I feel a great sense of peace. I feel that I am in alignment with the universe. I am not isolated, but a part of the whole."

Spontaneously, we formed a circle. With our arms around each other, we stood and swayed. We cried and we laughed. As we looked at each other lovingly, our voices rose in a jubilant sound.

Class was over.

RECOMMENDED READING

Bach, George. *Creative Aggression*. New York: Avon, 1967.

————. *The Intimate Enemy*. New York: Avon, 1970.

> Excellent books on how to fight and why we need to.

Bean, Orson. *Me and the Orgone*. Connecticut: Fawcett Publications, 1971.

> A touching, humorous story of one man's experience with Reichian therapy.

Feldenkrais, Moshe. *Awareness Through Movement*. New York: Harper and Row, 1977.

> Contains a brief, brilliant explanation of Feldenkrais's technique as well as twelve exciting exercises.

————. *Body and Mature Behavior*. New York: International Universities Press, 1975.

> Difficult but brilliant explanation of how the brain and the body are connected.

Freud, Sigmund. *The Ego and the Id*. New York: Norton Library, 1963.

——— . *Sexuality and the Psychology of Love*. New York: Collier Books, 1963.

Two germinal works expounding the theories which Reich was later to explore.

Gallwey, Timothy. *The Inner Game of Tennis*. New York: Random House, 1974.

Techniques to help you stop trying and simply become aware.

Horney, Karen. *Neurosis and Human Growth*. New York: W.W. Norton and Co., 1950.

A humanistic view of how our self-image gets in our way.

Linklater, Kristan. *Freeing the Natural Voice*. New York: Drama Books, 1976.

Exercises for freeing the voice.

Lowen, Alexander. *The Betrayal of the Body*. New York: Collier Books, 1967.

——— . *Pleasure*. London: Penguin Books, 1977.

——— . *Bioenergetics*. New York: Penguin, 1976.

The best popular explanations of Reichian theory. How armoring affects the body.

Perls, Frederick. *Gestalt Therapy Verbatim*. Utah: Real People Press, 1969.

Transcripts of Perls at work.

———— . *Gestalt Therapy*. New York: Bantam, 1977.

A series of exercises for physical/emotional/mental self-exploration.

Reich, Wilhelm. *Character Analysis*. New York: Simon and Schuster, 1972.

———— . *The Function of the Orgasm*. New York: Simon and Schuster, 1973.

Difficult reading but interesting.

Stanislavsky, Konstantin. *An Actor Prepares*. New York: Theatre Arts Books, 1947.

Still the best book on acting. Much to say about making choices and going after what you want.

Steiner, Claude. *Scripts People Live*. New York: Bantam Books, 1974.

How we choose our patterns of living and then get stuck in them.

Todd, Mabel Ellsworth. *The Thinking Body*. New York: Dance Horizons, 1968.

The best book around on the human skeleton and how it works.